SOUTHERN YOSEMITE

ROCK CLIMBS

SOUTHERN
YOSEMITE

ROCK

CLIMBS

MARK AND SHIRLEY SPENCER

Published by:
Condor Designs
P. O. Box 1629
Oakhurst, CA 93644

ISBN 0-9620158-0-6

CONDOR DESIGNS

New route information, corrections or comments should be sent to:

Mark Spencer
P.O Box 1629
Oakhurst, CA 93644

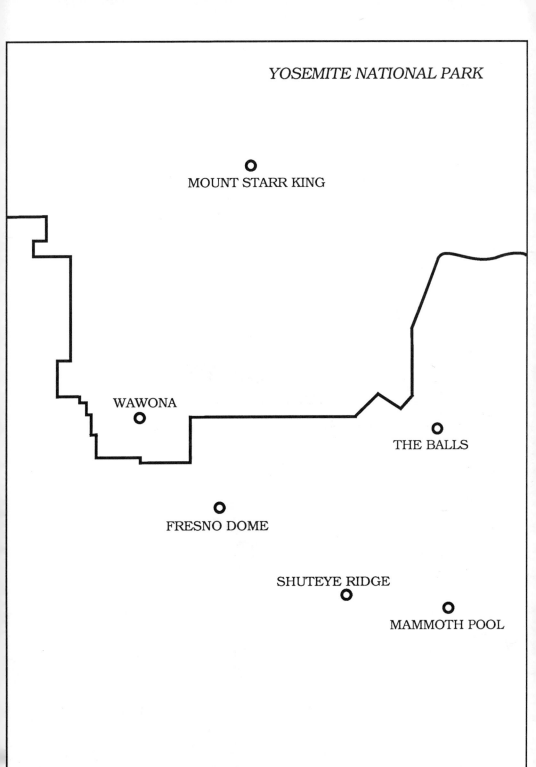

TABLE OF CONTENTS

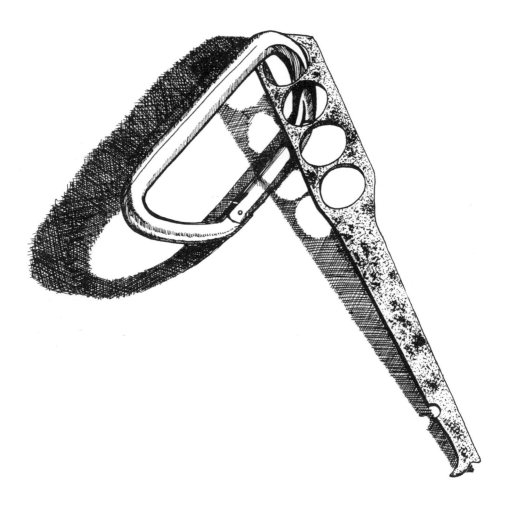

PREFACE

For many years now, word has been quietly circulating of the superb and remote rock south of Yosemite Valley. However, most climbers have been baffled by a general lack of accurate climbing information for this area. The 1976 High Sierra Climbing Guide listed several of the domes in the region, but was more an overview than a definitive guide. The 1971 Yosemite Climbing Guide listed several climbs for Mt. Starr King, but later editions relegated it to an index. In 1984 a small Wawona Rock guide appeared, but went out of print quickly. From time to time magazine articles have appeared, along with American Alpine Journal entries, but route descriptions tended to be quite vague. Some of the climbers active in the area neglected to record their ascents. Some closely guarded their information in an effort to keep the area secret. Unfortunately, this practice resulted in some climbs receiving multiple "first ascents". Many domes in the region carry multiple names, bestowed by each successive "discoverer". Sorting out all of this obscure and sometimes conflicting information has been no easy task. Fortunately, many climbers active in this area have contributed a significant amount of information to this effort. Special thanks are due: Alan Bartlett, Brett Bernhardt, Jim Cunningham, Jack Delk, Gary Fluitt, Tom Higgins, Simon King, Vaino Kodas, Mike Mayer, Steve McCabe, Alan Nelson, Royal Robbins, Don Timmer, and Greg Vernon. Their efforts to make this book as complete and accurate as possible are very much appreciated. It is the purpose of this book to preserve the history and climbs of this wild and beautiful area, so special to us all.

INTRODUCTION

Along the west slope of the Sierra, a host of domes and outcrops lie hidden among the pines. In contrast to the sheer power of the great walls of Yosemite Valley, the subtle elegance of the Southern Yosemite domes have often been overlooked by all but the most inquisitive eyes. The curious few have been generously rewarded by some of the most beautiful and pristine climbing in the range. Climbing here is more an act of discovery than just climbing a set of holds. The vast amount of granite, and the wilderness character of the Southern Yosemite area will no doubt provide the same rewards for many years to come.

The many domes in Southern Yosemite are widely scattered, with each making up its own unique climbing area. Most of the domes are located in Sierra National Forest. Many climbs lie close to the road with approaches of 15 minutes or less. Some require up to an hour to approach and a few climbs such as routes on Bunnell Point and Balloon Dome require a day to approach.

May through November generally see the best climbing weather. By the end of November early snows often close the high mountain roads and make small handholds viciously slick and hard to climb. In early May enough snow has melted from the high roads to allow passage. However, as early as March wild-eyed diehards can be spotted crashing through snowdrifts enroute to their favorite crags. In low snow years, any time is the right time to climb. It is always good to check in at the Forest Service in Oakhurst for road conditions and closures before driving up in early season. The phone number at the Ranger Station is 209-683-4665.

STYLE AND ETHICS

The issues of style and ethics have always been an intrinsic part of climbing. Style can be defined as the particular method that a climber uses to ascend the rock. This book does not presume to dictate the style in which one must climb. Climbing must be preserved as a very personal and esthetic activity; the most meaningful method of ascent. We should not feel compelled to keep up with the French, or be pressured to climb without the "taint" of chalk, bolts, shoes, or ropes. We should of course, have respect for those who climbed here before us and those who will climb after us. Ethics therefore define this relationship of climbers to each other. Since the rocks belong to us all we should remember some important points:

1. Be respectful of other climbers. A carelessly dislodged rock can have dire consequences for those below. Don't assume that you are alone on the rock.
2. Climb safely. A good climb does not equal a dangerous climb. While free solo climbing is a rewarding climbing style, it is not for everyone. After all, many people do like to climb just for fun without the risk of death and disfigurement.
3. Many bolts on these climbs are 10 - 15 years old. Treat them accordingly. Some climbers put only single bolts at belays. We should all feel free to install double or triple belay bolts with 5/16" or 3/4" bolts. Likewise, if bolts on any of the routes look weak, they should be replaced with new stronger ones. When replacing these bolts, pull the bolt straight out of the hole and enlarge the hole for the new bolt.
4. Stylistic disputes can turn slanderous and ugly, sometimes resulting in environmental damage. Complaints should be limited to the people involved, not the rocks. Remember, hacked rock and bent bolts form a permanent record of an individual's unsportsmanship.
5. Keep the rock clean of trash. This is a true wilderness climbing area. Bleached slings and tin cans found at the base of remote climbs ten years after the first ascents proves once again that trash does not just go away. It has to be picked up. By all pitching in and keeping the area clean we can ensure a pristine in which to climb.
6. Many of the streams in the Sierra have become infected with Giardia. In the more remote areas of Southern Yosemite the mountain streams still run pure and clean. It is up to all of us to conserve this precious resource.
7. With the dispersed camping policy in the Sierra National Forest, it is possible to camp at undeveloped sites close to many of the climbing areas. These sites are sure to see increased use resulting in greater environmental impact. Campsites must be kept litter free and proper sanitation must be used. Remember, no one wants to camp in an outhouse.

USE OF GUIDE

The climbs in this guide have been divided into 6 major areas with a separate chapter covering each one. Each chapter introduction gives area highlights, history, access, camping information, and the best seasons to climb. A map at the beginning of each chapter gives an overview of the location of the domes and their approaches. A graded list of climbs and the list of first ascents are found at the back of the book. Information on new routes, as well as confirmation of present ratings are always welcome. Correspondence should be sent to the authors at the address in the front of the book.

WARNING

There are several factors that must be considered when climbing in the Southern Yosemite area. First, we must share the area with the native residents. Bears have a way of making a mess of improperly stored food. Keep food locked away in your car trunk, or if backpacking hung high in a tall tree. The bears tend to be more aggressive within the boundary of Yosemite National Park, however they frequent the National Forest as well. Rattlesnakes are common at lower elevations, especially in the summer. When walking through the thick brush, common throughout the Shuteye and Mammoth Pool areas, watch where you walk. One snakebite could spoil your whole day. Another summer hazard is wildfires, be careful with your campfire. In extreme fire hazard conditions the Forest Service may close certain access roads in the National Forest. Such hazard areas should be clearly posted, and during these times it is usually too hot to climb anyway. When Fall arrives and it seems safe to go back into the woods, guess again. Hunting season in the National Forest typically begins the third Saturday in September and runs for three weeks. There is also a one week season in mid to late October. During this time it would be wise to wear loud colors when walking through the woods. Don't let the hunters mistake you for big game. Finally, it must be stressed that this book is only a collection of route descriptions, not an instructional manual. Climbing is a sport that requires good personal judgement, a book is no substitute. If a route looks unsafe, remember, no one is forcing you to climb it.

RATINGS

The climbs in this book are rated according to the Yosemite Decimal System. Conforming to the popular custom, climbs above 5.10 are divided into a, b, c, and d sub-gradings whenever possible. It should be remembered, however, that some of these climbs are over ten years old and may have not seen second ascents. The ratings suggested by the first ascent parties are utilized and whenever possible confirmed or adjusted by subsequent ascenders. Aid gradings as well as length gradings are also included in this book. An explanation of these grades are as follows:

A1 Bolt or other solid easy aid placement. Also rappels or pendulums.
A2 More difficult, less secure placements.
A3 Difficult placement that will hold a short fall only.
A4 Placement will hold body weight only.
A5 Enough A4 placements to produce a 50'-60' fall.
Note: many of the aid climbs in this book were done well before today's active camming protection became available. Friends, TCU's, and Quickies will no doubt make these aid climbs cleaner and safer.

Grade I   A Short 1-2 pitch climb (in this book Grade I climbs do not carry the I prefix).
Grade II   A Climb of 2-5 pitches that will take 2-4 hours.
Grade III   A climb of 4-9 pitches that will take a half day or more.
Grade IV   A long more committing climb 7-12 pitches long requiring a full day to complete.
Grade V   A sustained 10 or more pitch climb requiring an overnight bivouac.
Grade VI   Generally a serious wall climb requiring two or more bivouacs.
Note: The longest climb in this book is Grade IV, although walls with the potential for longer routes do exist.

FREE RATINGS COMPARED

YDS	FRENCH	UIAA	AUSTRALIAN	ENGLISH
5.0		III	4	
5.1		III+	5	
5.2		IV-	6	3a
5.3		IV	7	3b
5.4		IV+	8-9	3c
5.5		V-	10-11	4a
5.6	4c	V	12-13	4b
5.7	5a	V+	14-15	4c
5.8	5b	VI-	16	4c/5a
5.9	5c	VI	17	5a
5.10a	5c+	VI+	18	5a/5b
5.10b	6a	VII-	19	5b
5.10c	6a+	VII	20	5b/5c
5.10d	6b	VII+	21	5c
5.11a	6b+	VII+	22	5c/6a
5.11b	6c	VIII-	23	6a
5.11c	6c+	VIII	24	6a/6b
5.11d	7a	VIII+	25	6b
5.12a	7a+	IX-	26	6b/6c
5.12b	7b	IX	27	6c
5.12c	7b+	IX+	28	6c/7a
5.12d	7c	IX+	29	7a
5.13a	7c+	X-	30	7a/7b
5.13b	8a	X	31	7b

TOPO LEGEND

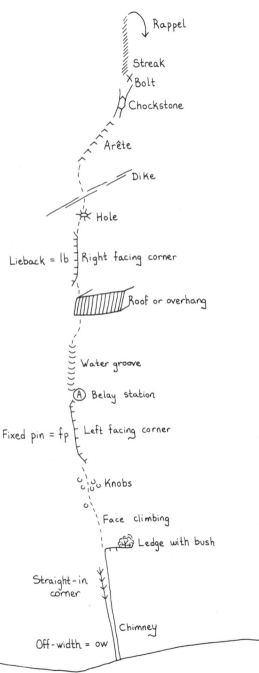

- Rappel
- Streak
- Bolt
- Chockstone
- Arête
- Dike
- Hole
- Lieback = lb — Right facing corner
- Roof or overhang
- Water groove
- (A) Belay station
- Fixed pin = fp — Left facing corner
- Knobs
- Face climbing
- Ledge with bush
- Straight-in corner
- Chimney
- Off-width = ow

MOUNT
STARR KING

CHAPTER 1

Mount Starr King is actually the northernmost of a group of three domes, set back in the forest three miles south of Yosemite Valley. While the Valley sees thousands of climbers every year, Mount Starr King usually sees 10 to 20 ascents per season. With a five mile hike in and a vast brushfield standing sentry below the dome, Starr King should remain a sanctuary of solitude for many years to come. From a backcountry campsite near the dome the view of the blazing evening alpenglow on the surrounding peaks can be a magical experience.

Although the north and south faces of Mount Starr King were first climbed over 100 years ago, climbing activity has taken place at a relatively slow pace. Most parties continue to climb the classic **Northeast Face** II 5.4 and the **Southeast Face** II 5.5 routes. In 1969, John Roebig, Ron Schroeder, and Tom Distler climbed a long curving lieback on the hidden east face at 5.7. The next year in 1970, Ken Boche with Lee Panza and later Mary Bomba began exploring the large open west face with routes directly up the face at 5.8 and the **Northwest** face at 5.9. Boche returned in 1972 with Tim Harrison to climb **Nuts and Bolts** III 5.8 on the west face. Several years later, in 1987, on a trip to research the climbs in the area, Mark Spencer climbed **Beast of Burden** II 5.9 and free soloed the striking **Tsunami** II 5.7, both on the east face of Mount Starr King. Meanwhile, several other parties wandered up the southern portion of the west face for 5-8 pitches at mild 5th class. Each party seems to have taken a different route. Other parties have climbed moderate to difficult 5th class routes on the nearby faces but the exact locations of the climbs and even which domes were climbed remain unknown.

The closest approach to Mount Starr King begins at the Mono Meadow trailhead on the Glacier Point Road, 11 miles from Chinquapin. A good trail leads 3 miles to Illilouette Creek. Good campsites can be found near the creek which is also the last source of water during most normal snow years. If you plan on camping here overnight, remember to pick up a wilderness permit at a ranger station first. Also, bears patrol the campsites nightly, so make sure to hang your food high. From Illilouette Creek, follow the maze of trails to the slopes leading up to the dome. Beware of the killer manzanita here which protects the dome above from unwary climbers. For routes on the west or northwest faces hike up the long ridge northwest of the dome and work back over to the start of the climbs. For routes on the east face and southeast saddle, leave the trail at a creek and hike up the slope to the saddle between the center and south peaks of Mount Starr King. Once at the saddle, hike north over the center peak to the start of the climbs.

With an elevation of 9092' the climbing season is generally from June through October. Several early season ascents have been made by climbers hiking or skiing in on the spring snowpack. If the snow still covers the brush this approach could be a good alternative. By mid-June the trails are usually snow-free and usually remain so until the early winter snowfalls of late October or early November. **NOTE**: The access to Mono Meadow trailhead is controlled by the condition of the Glacier Point Road which is closed in the winter. In early or late season it is best to call for park road conditions to make sure the Glacier Point Road is open.

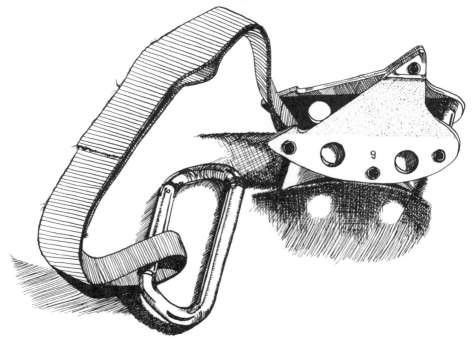

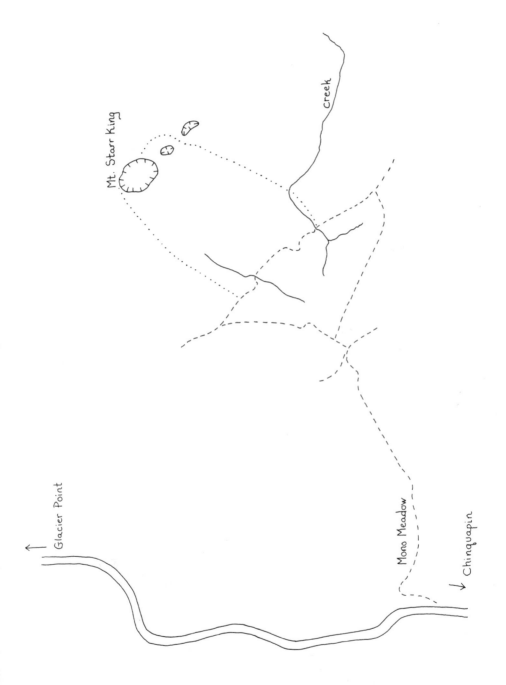

MOUNT STARR KING

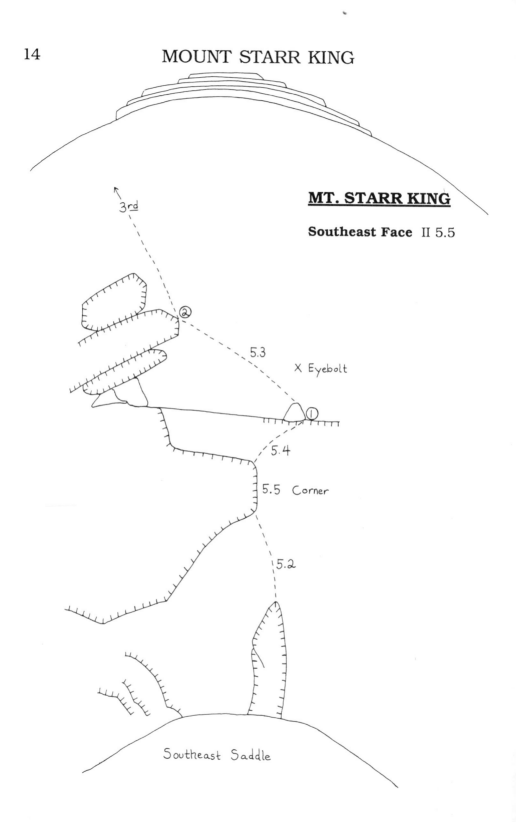

MT. STARR KING

Southeast Face II 5.5

3rd

5.3

X Eyebolt

5.4

5.5 Corner

5.2

Southeast Saddle

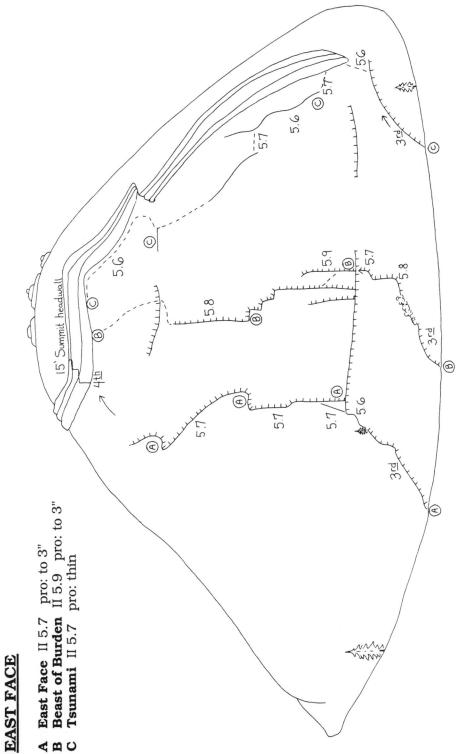

EAST FACE

A **East Face** II 5.7 pro: to 3"
B **Beast of Burden** II 5.9 pro: to 3"
C **Tsunami** II 5.7 pro: thin

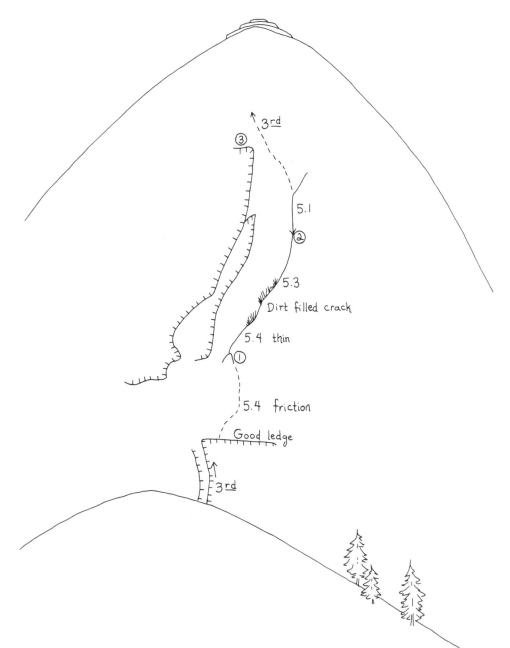

MT. STARR KING

Northeast Face II 5.4   pro: to 3"
Begin at the highest point of the shoulder on the Northeast Face.

WEST FACE

Northwest Face III 5.9   Begin on the northwest face, below a series of green, lichen covered overhangs, 100 feet up. Climb the left of a pair of twin cracks up and left for two pitches. After the second pitch, climb up and right to a double bolt belay. Climb 5.9 friction for 15 feet up and right to a bolt. Continue up past one more bolt to a small belay ledge. Two more 5.9 pitches lead up the face to a wide crack. Follow the crack up and right then cut back left (5.9) to the summit slabs. Pro to 2"

Nuts and Bolts III 5.8   In the center of the west face is a high prow capped by a pine tree. Begin 200 feet left and climb a third class pitch to a flake. From the flake, climb up 5.8 friction past several bolts to a good ledge. The difficulty eases above with several more moderate pitches leading to the summit.

West Face III 5.8   Spot a row of three jeffrey pines at the base of the west face. Begin just to the left at a bent lodgepole pine and follow a water trough up and right to a belay bolt. Go right (5.8) then up and right to a brushy ledge. Climb up and right for two more pitches before traversing 30 feet right then up past loose flakes to a good ledge. Climb up more flakes and past a few small overhangs for three more pitches to the summit.

BUNNELL POINT

Northwest Face IV 5.9
This fine face route takes on the remote northwest face of Bunnell Point, which towers high over the upper end of Little Yosemite Valley. Begin climbing just right of the center of the northwest face, at a large tree. Two prominent dikes slant up and left, joining halfway up the face. Follow the right dike up to the left edge of a long, thin roof. Continue up past the roof and up and left into a vague, broken right facing corner which leads to the top. There are 15 bolts to protect the climb's 14 pitches. Beware of off route bolts around mid-height below the long thin roof.

Approach   The 10 mile hike up from Happy Isles to Lost Valley is both spectacular and strenuous. Wilderness permits are required for overnight camping in Little Yosemite. The area is often crowded and permits are scarce, so plan ahead. Campsites in the Little Yosemite Campground feature pit toilets and steel bear boxes, a great convenience in securing precious food from the pesky campground raiders. For those who appreciate a little solitude, good campsites without the bear boxes can be found farther upstream, closer to Bunnell Point. Be sure to treat all water in the area for giardia. In low water, the river can be forded in several places below Bunnell Point. During the Spring runoff, however cross the river on a bridge above Bunnell Cascade and work back to the base of the northwest face.

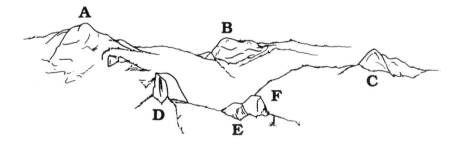

A	Clouds Rest	**D**	Half Dome
B	Bunnell Point	**E**	Mount Broderick
C	Mount Starr King	**F**	Liberty Cap

Benny chalks up.

WAWONA

CHAPTER 2

Wawona, located just 25 miles south of Yosemite Valley, continues to be a quiet backwater of Southern Yosemite climbing. Wawona Dome provides a spectacular backdrop for the many small cliffs scattered throughout the area. The Pioneer History Center provides an interesting look at Yosemite history, and the Wawona Hotel with its golf course can provide the most scenic 9 holes of golf anywhere (with the added bonus of deer on the fairway).

Climbing history here has always been closely linked with Camp Wawona, a summer camp located at the end of Forest Drive. Founded in 1929, the camp has a long tradition of hiking and climbing activities. In the 1960s Earl Tressenriter, along with others established several short aid lines in the Icehouse area as well as early routes on Wawona Dome. During the 1980s the emphasis shifted to short free lines on the lower cliffs pioneered primarily by Wawona locals Mark and Shirley Spencer. During the summer season they were joined by fellow Camp Wawona climbing instructors Floyd Hayes, Kevin Wilcox, Dwight Simpson, and Bob Neal. Together they established many short testpieces such as **Firefly** 5.11a, **Yellow Banana** 5.10b, **Cornerstone** 5.11a, and **Atlantis** 5.11b at Icehouse, as well as several new routes on Wawona Dome, including the 1985 free ascent of Fred Beckey's 1970 route to produce **Blue Moon** III 5.11b. Wawona has also seen extensive bouldering activity, in fact the majority of the climbers spend most of their time at the bouldering areas scattered throughout Wawona. This chapter includes several of the most popular boulders.

Wawona is located in Yosemite National Park, on highway 41, six miles north of the South Entrance. Allow one hour from Yosemite Valley and 45 minutes from Oakhurst. Year round camping can be found at the Wawona Campground one mile north of the historic Wawona Hotel. Sites are first come first served which usually presents no problem except during the high summer tourist season. Forest Service campsites are available just outside the Park but the problem of repaying entrance fees every time you go out limits their appeal. A great campsite above Chilnualna Falls provides 30 minute access to routes on Wawona Dome. To get there, drive two miles up Chilnualna Road to the Clilnualna Falls Trailhead. Hike 4 miles up the trail to a trail junction. Good campsites can be found near the creek, just below some spectacular cascades. To get to Wawona Dome, cross the creek (difficult in spring) and hike south and down to the gap between the main dome and the northern wall containing Miwok and Chulook. A wilderness permit is required for backcountry camping and is available at the Ranger Station in Wawona.

March to November are the best months for climbing in Wawona. With a base elevation of 4000 feet, the lower cliffs offer year round climbing, with only a few weeks lost to winter snows. In spring and early summer, climbs near the waterfalls are usually to wet to climb, although the nearby clothing optional swimming areas provide a pleasant distraction. High summer temperatures often top 90 degrees making mid-day swim breaks mandatory. Fall brings cooler temperatures along with brilliant fall colors.

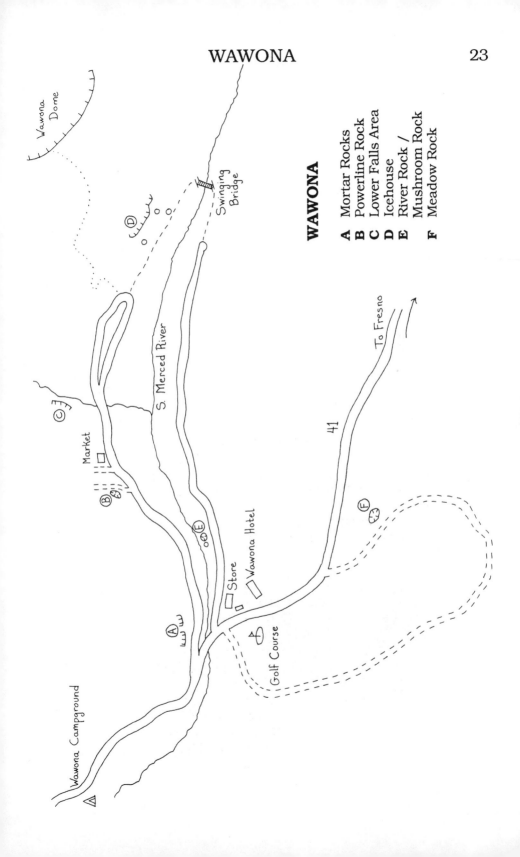

WAWONA

A Mortar Rocks
B Powerline Rock
C Lower Falls Area
D Icehouse
E River Rock /
    Mushroom Rock
F Meadow Rock

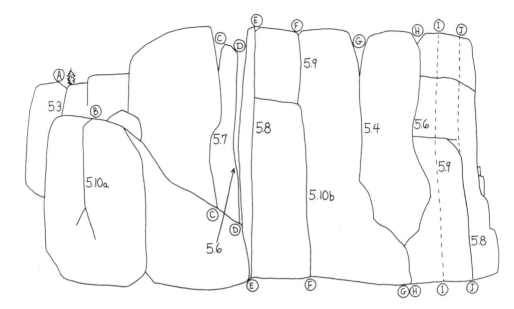

MORTAR ROCK

The Mortar Rocks provide convenient roadside bouldering. From Highway 41 turn onto Chilnualna road and drive for .1 mile. The Mortar Rocks can be identified as the tiny outcrops on the north side of the road just before the first houses. Manzanita bushes on top of the rocks provide good top rope anchors for those who don't like hard landings from the higher problems.

A	5.3	Easy crack
B	5.10a	Thin crack / overhang
	5.9	If you jump
C	5.7	Face climbing
D	5.6	Hand crack
E	5.8	Fist crack
F	5.10b	Thin crack
G	5.4	Crack / lieback
H	5.6	Crack / lieback
I	5.9	Face between cracks
J	5.8	Thin crack / lieback/ mantle

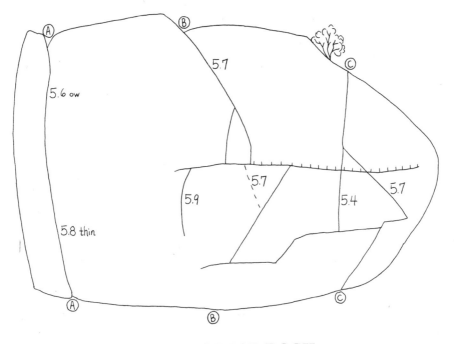

EAST MORTAR ROCK

This 20' rock lies just east of the main Mortar Rock. A top rope anchor can easily be fixed from the top of the rock for safety. In addition to the listed routes, other short problems can be found on the boulders scattered on the hillside above.

A 5.8   Thin crack that turns offwidth near the top.

B 5.7   Climb up to a small ledge, then lieback up and left.
    5.9   Variation: A difficult mantle gains the initial small ledge.

C 5.7   Climb the awkward dogleg crack on the right side.
    5.4   Variation: An easy crack avoids the dogleg difficulties.

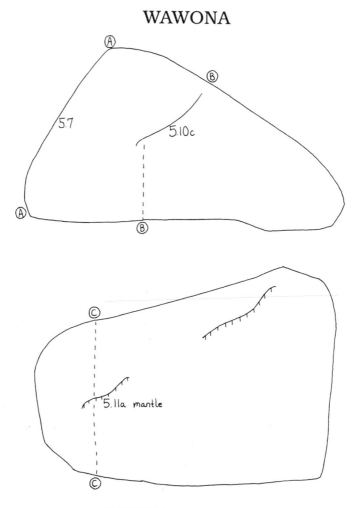

POWERLINE ROCK

This boulder is located in North Wawona, near the Pine Tree Market. From Highway 41, drive 1.5 miles east on Chilnualna road. About 200 feet before the Pine Tree Market, turn left (north) on a paved road. The rock is on the left side of the road, directly under a powerline.

A   Electron 5.7
Climb the northwest corner of the rock.

B   High Voltage 5.10c
On the west face, opposite the road, face climb to the shallow crack, then up and over the rounded edge to the top.

C   Power Failure 5.11a
This steep white face which fronts on the road provides a good power mantle workout.

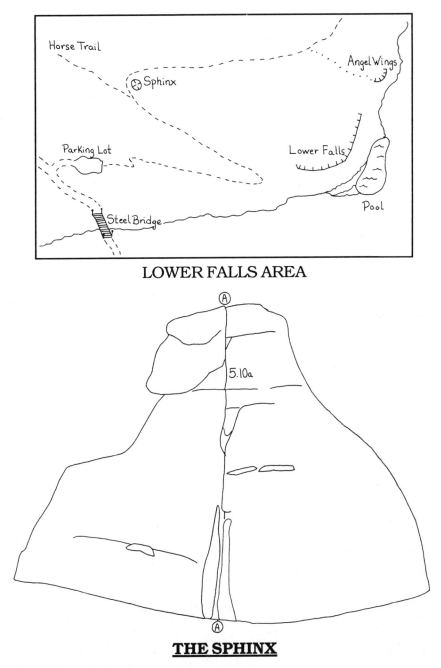

LOWER FALLS AREA

THE SPHINX

A   Sphinx Crack   5.10a   pro: friends #1-#3

Approach   Walk up the Chilnualna Falls trail for about 1/2 mile to the junction of the horse path on the left. Continue on the Falls trail for 10 more yards. The Sphinx can be seen to the right just above the trail.

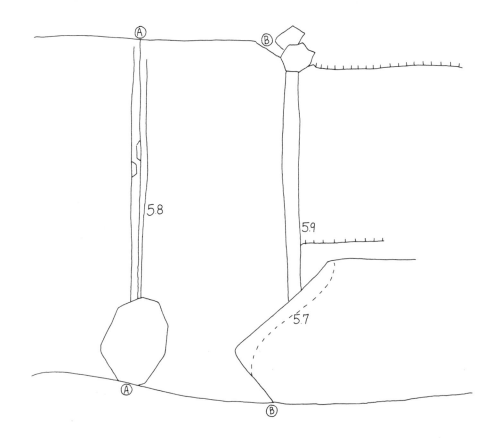

LOWER FALLS

A Hanging Garden Crack 5.8
B Circus of Values 5.9

Approach From the Chilnualna Falls trailhead walk up the trail for 1/4 mile to the lower falls and cascades. At the point where the main trail switches back and left up the hill, a series of stone steps lead up and right. Follow these steps for a short distance to where they pass directly below a steep, black 60' cliff. The best time to climb here is in mid summer to early fall when the water is at lower levels.

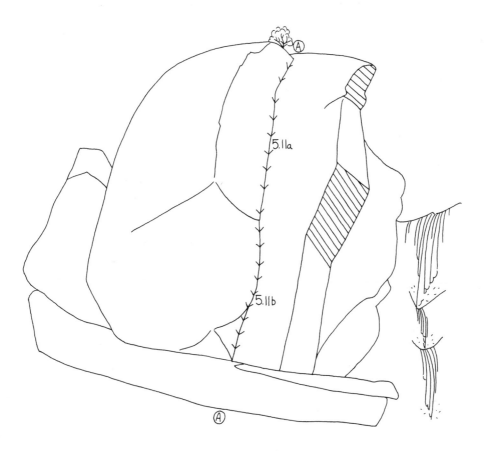

ANGEL WINGS

A   Angel Wings 5.11b

Approach   From the climbs at the Lower Falls it is possible to work up the cascades to a large pool (good swimming on hot summer days). Angel Wings can be seen on the buttress that is just left of the cascade that feeds the pool. In early season this approach is unpassable due to high water. An alternate approach follows the Chilnualna Falls trail for 1 mile to a sandy bench that overlooks the creek. Good paths lead south for 200 yards to the top of the Angel Wings Buttress. Work right (west) down a broken up area to the base.

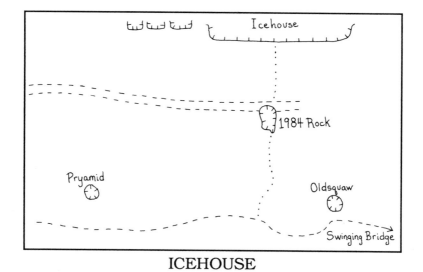

ICEHOUSE

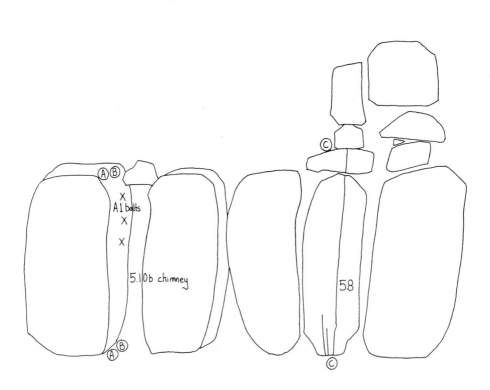

ICEHOUSE

A Pilgrims Progress A1
B Atlas 5.10b (Pilgrims Progress free)
C Old and Wise 5.8 Pro: thin
D Yellow Banana 5.10b pro: friends #1-#3.5
E Cornerstone 5.11a pro: tri-cams #.5-#1.5

Approach From the Chilnualna Falls trailhead at the end of the Chilnualna Road, continue on the dirt road down a small hill and across the steel bridge that crosses Chilnualna Creek. After the last house the dirt road turns into a trail leading to the Swinging Bridge. Follow the trail a few hundered yards into an open meadow. From this meadow, Icehouse can be identified as the 100 foot high cliffband on the hillside above.

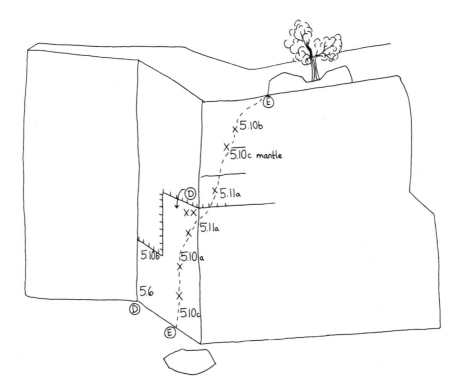

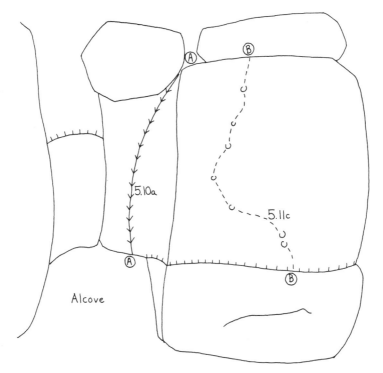

ICEHOUSE

A   Thompson Harmonizer 5.10a
B   Nubbs 5.11c (TR)

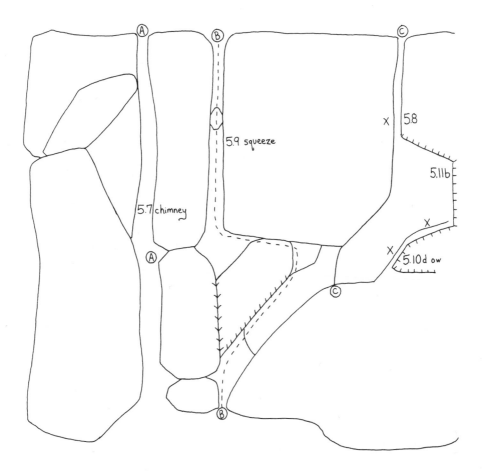

ICEHOUSE

A   **Double or Nothing** 5.7   pro: wide
B   **Galt's Gulch** 5.9
C   **Atlantis** 5.11b   pro: friends #1-#3

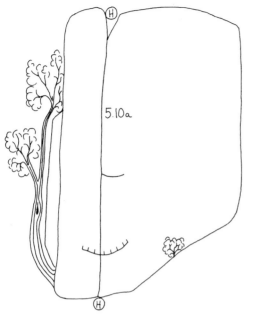

ICEHOUSE

H   Color Me Gone 5.10a
pro: tiny nuts to #2 friend

Approach   This climb is located
on a small buttress at the
extreme right end of Icehouse,
200 feet right of Atlantis.

1984 ROCK

A   Thought Police 5.5
Climb up the corner on several small
ledges.

B   Lieback Detector 5.8
Short steep lieback.

C   Newspeak 5.11c
Climb the thin mantle in the center of
the face.

D   Doublethink   5.11a
Climb the arete between Newspeak and
Big Brother.

Big Brother Face
E   Right 5.8   This is also the descent.
F   Center 5.8   Climb the face.
G   Left 5.7   Climb the arete.

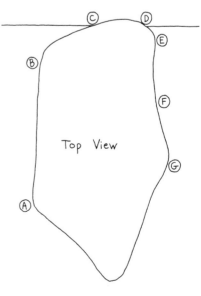

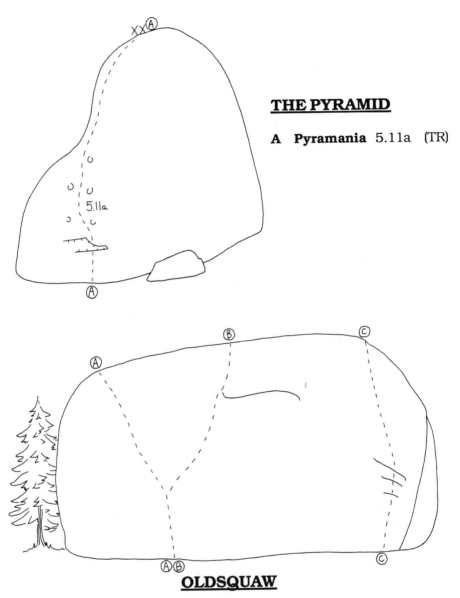

THE PYRAMID

A **Pyramania** 5.11a (TR)

OLDSQUAW

A	5.4	Climb up on large holds.
B	5.8	Climb up and right on smaller holds.
C	5.10d	Climb thin edges up the right side.

Approach Follow the swinging bridge trail to the meadow below Icehouse. From a brown Park Service sign, Oldsquaw is visible through the woods 100' to the east. The climbs are on the west face. The Pyramid lies at the northeast edge of the meadow 100 yards north of Oldsquaw, at the base of the hill leading up to Pilgrims Progress.

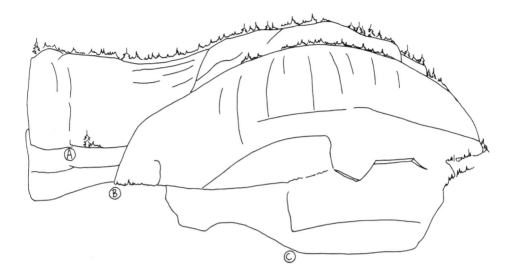

WAWONA DOME

A   Chulook II 5.9
       Boulevard of Dreams II 5.8
       Miwok II 5.7

B   Hazy Days II 5.10a
       Welcome to Wawona II 5.9

C   Blue Moon II 5.11b

Approach

From the Chilnualna Falls parking lot walk across the steel bridge to the end
of the dirt road 200 yards further. Just past the last house on the road a faint
fire road leads left, up the hillside. A chain across the road with a fire road
sign provides a good landmark for the correct path. Hike up the washed out
roadbed always keeping to the left at road forks. Follow this road for 2 miles
until it terminates just below the face of Wawona Dome. A short brushy
scramble leads to the beginning of the climbs. Allow 1 1/2 hours for this
approach. An alternate approach can be made from the top of Chilnualna
Falls. From the campsite mentioned in the chapter introduction, cross the
creek and scramble south to the top of the dome. Descend the gully between
the main dome and the north wall containing Miwok and Chulook. Allow 2
1/2 to 3 hours for this approach from the parking lot. This route is more
often used for a descent from the top of the dome.

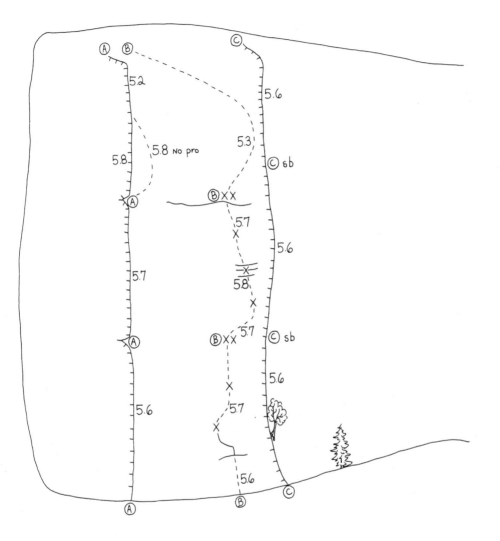

WAWONA DOME - NORTH WALL

A   Chulook II 5.9   pro: to 4"
B   Boulevard of Dreams II 5.8   pro: to 1"
C   Miwok II 5.7   pro: to 3"

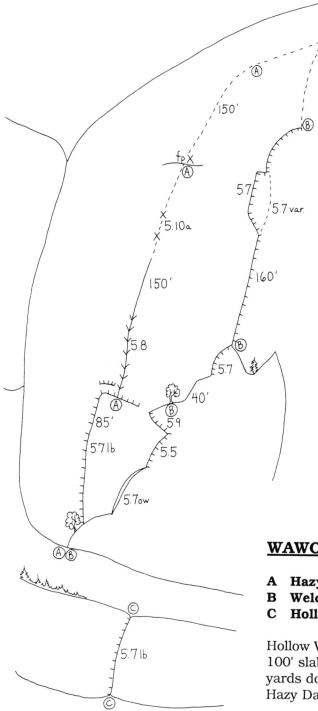

WAWONA DOME

A   Hazy Days II 5.10a
B   Welcome to Wawona II 5.9
C   Hollow Wallow 5.7

Hollow Wallow is located on a
100' slab, several hundered
yards down and right from
Hazy Days.

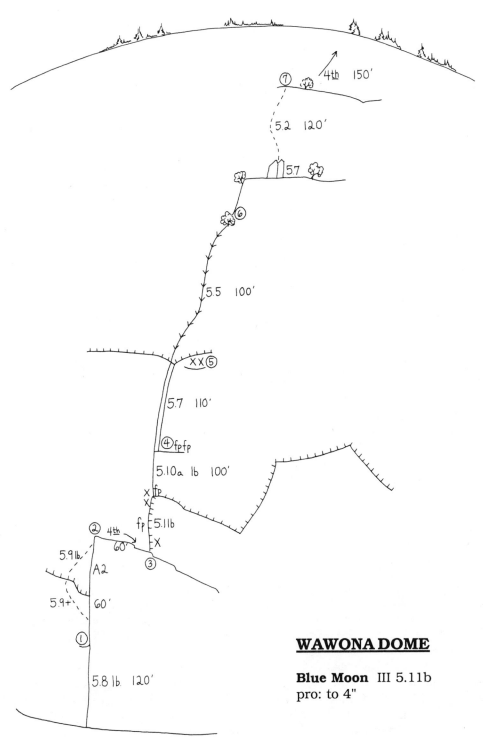

4th 150'

⑦

5.2 120'

5.7

⑥

5.5 100'

XX⑤

5.7 110'

④ fp fp

5.10a lb 100'

X fp
X

fp 5.11b

② 4th
60'

5.9 lb

X

③

A2

5.9+

60'

①

5.8 lb 120'

WAWONA DOME

Blue Moon III 5.11b
pro: to 4"

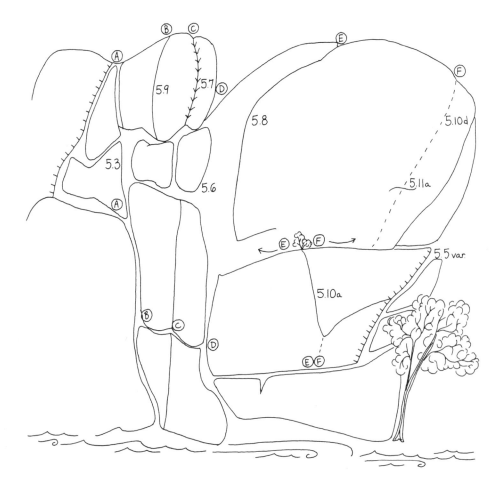

RIVER ROCK

A **Worm Squirm** 5.4
B **On The Edge** 5.9 (TR)
C **Alcove Overhang** 5.7
D **Green Slime** 5.6
E **Wise Crack** 5.10a
F **Firefly** 5.11a (TR)

Approach The River Rock is a 35' granite cliff that overlooks the river 100 yards upstream from the covered bridge at the Pioneer History Center. Drive up Forest Drive to the first hill and park off the pavement on the left, overlooking the river. Mushroom Rock is a small outcrop attached to the west side of River Rock.

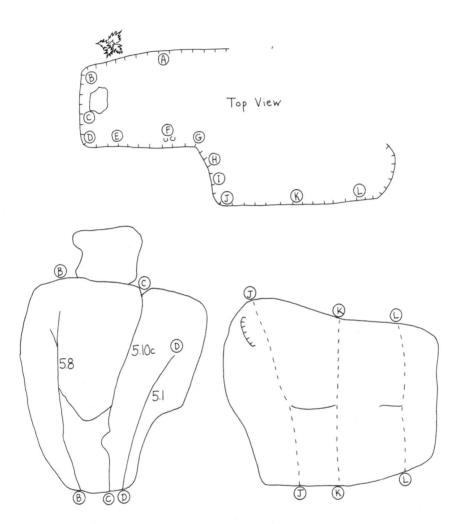

<u>MUSHROOM ROCK</u>

A	5.3	Climb the crack	**G**	5.8	Mantle in corner
B	**Sleeping Moss** 5.8		**H**	5.8+	Mantle
C	**Turning Green** 5.10c		**I**	5.9	Mantle
D	**Chute Out** 5.1		**J**	5.9	Mantle/Lieback
E	5.3	Climb up and right	**K**	5.9	Mantle on small knobs
F	5.8+	Mantle on knobs only	**L**	5.8	Mantle on small Knobs

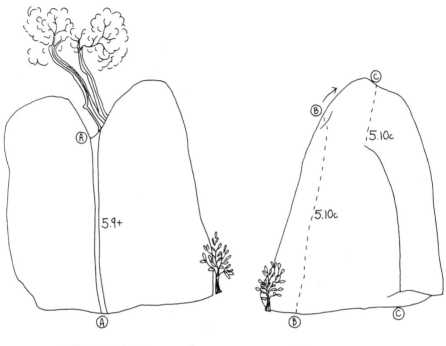

WEST FACE   SOUTH FACE

MEADOW ROCK

A **Bad Animal** 5.9+
B **Lieback Route** 5.10c (TR)
C **Hula Hoop** 5.10c (TR)

Approach   From Wawona, drive south on highway 41 for .7 of a mile. As the road leaves the golf course and climbs the wooded hillside, the Meadow rock will be visible to the south or downhill side of the road. The large oak growing from the top of the rock provides a sturdy top rope anchor.

Albert, happy about his good luck.

FRESNO DOME

CHAPTER 3

Rising above the forest in the hills above Oakhurst is the stately granite mass of Fresno Dome. Good roads lead up into the National Forest to a good campground at its base. Originally called Wa-mello by the Indians, mapmakers later changed the name to match the nearby Fresno Grove of Big Trees. Interestingly enough, the Fresno Big Trees were later renamed to honor John A. Nelder, a retired gold miner who settled in the grove in the 1860s and became the guardian of the trees. The name Wa-mello was misplaced and it has been known as Fresno Dome ever since.

Fresno Dome has seen extensive climbing activity, although because of its remote location, little history has survived. A bolt fixed in the Hawk Dome Gully bears the date 1953, but the first recorded ascent of the north face of Fresno Dome was by Fred Beckey and Jim Stuart in 1971. Royal Robbins led the first of his "Hinterlands" expeditions into the area in 1973 finding several routes on Watership Down and Zipa-De-Do-Da Buttress. For the next several years Robbins and his expedition members explored the area, climbing many fine routes on "Wamello Dome" as he was fond of calling it. Tom Higgins and Ruprecht Kammerlander visited the area in 1978 establishing their classic but runout 5.10c face route in the southwest face. Throughout the 1980s, several other climbers were active on the new route scene. Blaine Neeley added several lines on the south face, Jim Cunningham concentrated on the moderate classics and Mark and Shirley Spencer's exploration of the dome has been rewarded with many classic testpieces both on Fresno Dome and the Willow Creek Wall.

To reach Fresno Dome, follow highway 41 to the Skyranch Road (6S10), 4 miles north of Oakhurst. The paved road leads past the golf course and up into the National Forest. Drive 12 miles up the Skyranch road to a T junction. To get to Willow Creek Wall, turn right, toward Beasore Meadow and drive one mile. Willow Creek Wall is the prominent 100 ft. crag just north of the road. To continue to Fresno Dome turn left at the junction, following the signs to Fresno Dome campground, 2 miles further. Pass the junction of road 6S07 which goes left to Fish Camp 9 miles distant. This alternate route which is closer when driving south from Yosemite contains some rough road and three challenging creek crossings which may be impassible during spring runoff. Back at the junction of road 6S07, continue past the Fresno Dome campground up and around the north slope of Fresno Dome. At a point about 2 miles past the campground the road passes close to a creek on the right (south). Park here, cross the creek and pick up an old logging road that leads southwest up the back slope of the dome. Allow 15 minutes for this short hike. In early season when snow blocks the road on the north side of Fresno Dome, the south face may be approached from the vicinity of Fresno Dome Campground. Hike up the road toward the dome for a few hundred yards. At the first switchback (curving left) follow a faint logging road to the right into the woods. After a few hundered yards on this road, strike off left up the steep forested slope to the base of the south face. Allow 30 minutes for this approach.

The climbing season at Fresno Dome is typically controlled by the amount of snowfall blocking the road. Most of the climbs are south facing, permitting good climbing when the sun is out. Willow Creek Wall, at 6200' is located on a south facing road that is often snow free throughout much of the winter. The road up to the north slope of Fresno Dome holds a greater amount of snow which can block the road till mid-March or later if it is a high snow year. During the summer, the 7540' elevation provides comfortable climbing on all but the hottest days. Fall climbing typically lasts well into November until winter snows make the road impassable.

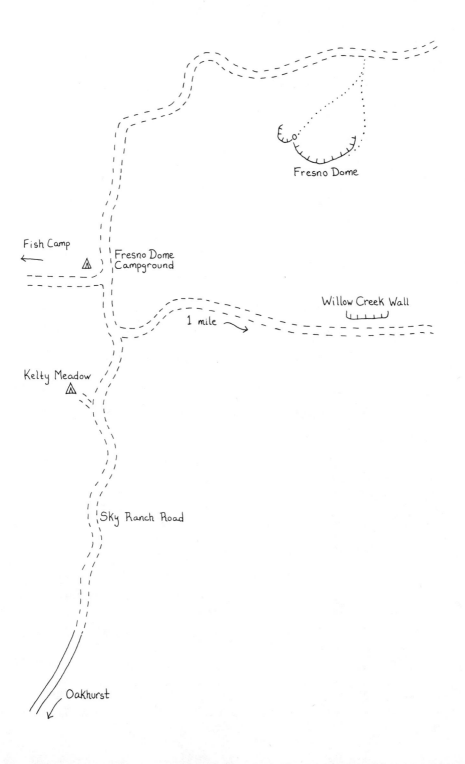

Fresno Dome

Fish Camp

Fresno Dome
Campground

Willow Creek Wall

1 mile

Kelty Meadow

Sky Ranch Road

Oakhurst

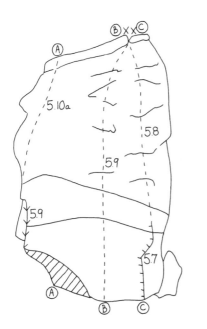

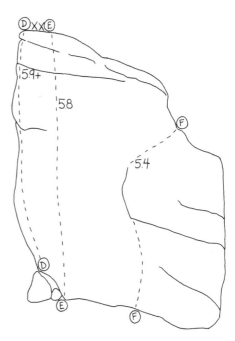

SOUTH FACE   EAST FACE

ERASERHEAD

A Rocky Road 5.10a
B Orange Peel 5.9
C Shakey Flakes 5.8
D The Prow 5.9+
E Cookie Slam 5.8
F Tin Roof 5.4

These short top rope routes are found on the small tower in the notch between Fresno Dome and Hawk Dome.

HAWK DOME

Hawk Dome is the prominent satellite dome attached to the west shoulder of Fresno Dome. Although not described here, several moderate to difficult routes have been established on its south face.

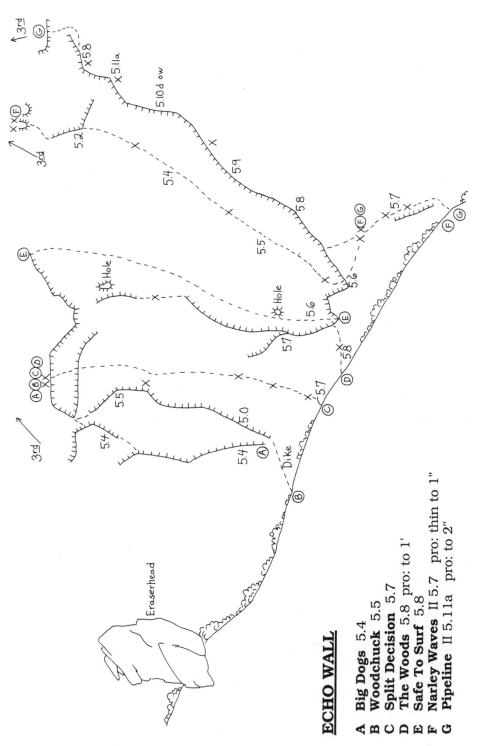

ECHO WALL

A **Big Dogs** 5.4
B **Woodchuck** 5.5
C **Split Decision** 5.7
D **The Woods** 5.8 pro: to 1'
E **Safe To Surf** 5.8
F **Narley Waves** II 5.7 pro: thin to 1"
G **Pipeline** II 5.11a pro: to 2"

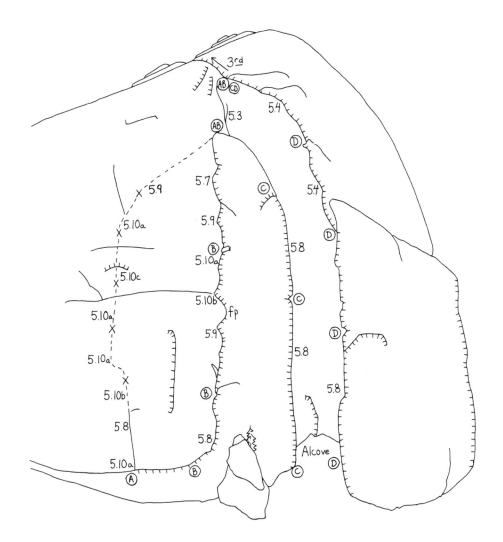

WEST FACE

A Kammerlander II 5.10c   runout
B The Predator II 5.10b   pro: to 4"
C Onyx II 5.8
D Buzzard Book II 5.8
E South Pillar II 5.7   (not illustrated)
Begin down and right of the Buzzard Book alcove. Climb onto the prominent
pillar and follow it up 4 pitches to the top of Fresno Dome.

SOUTH FACE

A   **Easy Wind** III 5.9
B   **Mule Train** II 5.7
C   **Ghastly Gulch** II 5.7

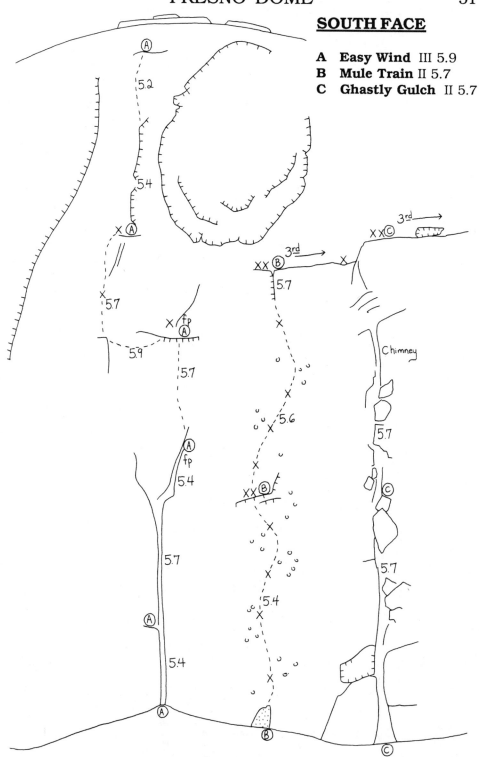

A **Friction Dandy** II 5.7
B **Looking Glass** II 5.7
C **Nuthanger** II 5.7
D **Rowsby Woof** III 5.8
E **Watership Down** III 5.7
F **Fresno Flats** III 5.8
G **Fox Trot** II 5.6

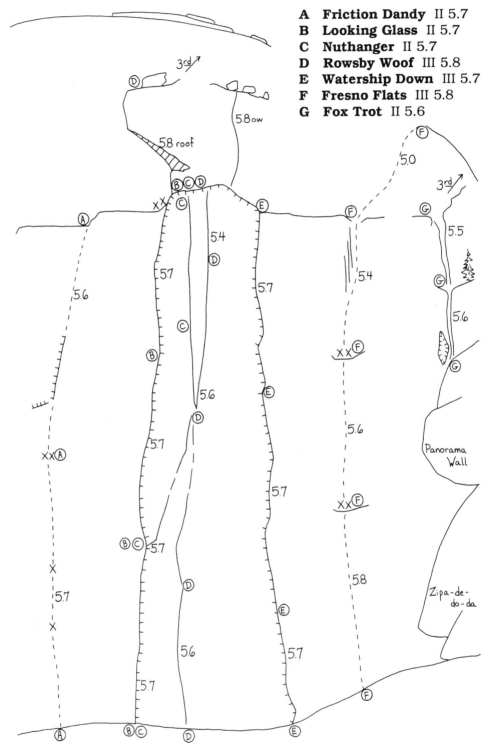

ZIPA-DE-DO-DA BUTTRESS

A Bay Bridge 5.6
B Golden Gate 5.7
C Trough 5.5
D Busy Bee 5.8
E Thin Spread 5.8
F Bypass 5.8
G Lay Away Flake 5.7
H Aurora 5.11d
I Beat Farmer 5.11d
J Hole in The Wall 5.10a
K Snowball 5.7

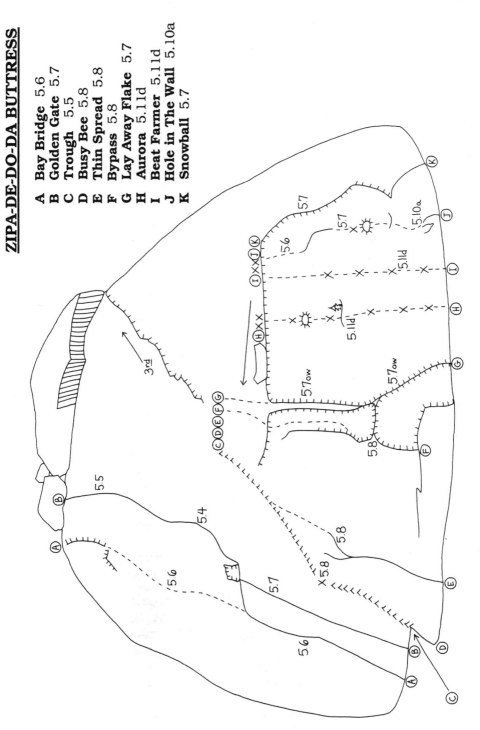

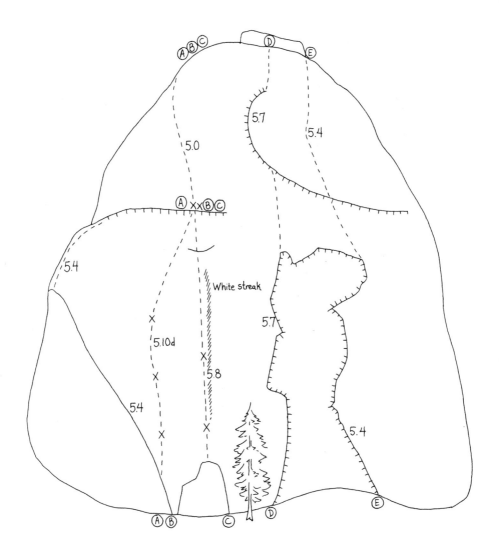

PANORAMA WALL

- **A Sink Me** 5.4
- **B Panorama** 5.10d
- **C Water Wheel** 5.8
- **D Fire and Ice** 5.7
- **E Morning Thunder** 5.4

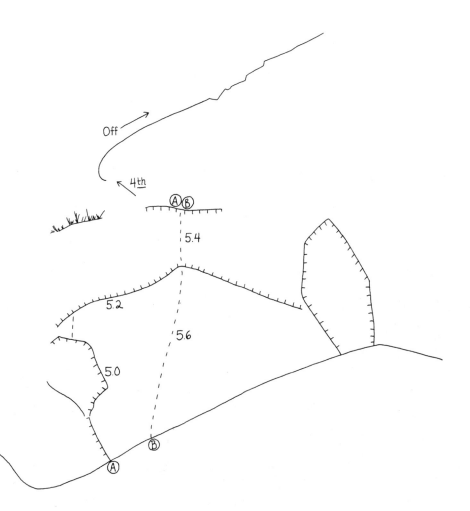

EAST FACE

A   **Made in the Shade** 5.3
B   **Arch Direct** 5.6

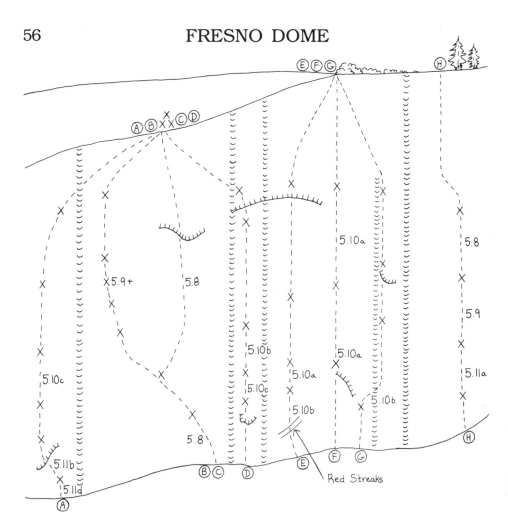

WILLOW CREEK WALL

A **Walk Of Life** 5.11d
B **Impatience** 5.9+
C **High Wire** 5.8 runout
D **Starched Shorts** 5.10c
E **Flamous** 5.10b
F **Talking Bear** 5.10a
G **Hoser** 5.10b
H **Easy Money** 5.11a

Approach   Willow Creek Wall is located 1 mile southeast of Fresno Dome. From Highway 41 follow the Skyranch Road for 12 miles. Just past the turnoff to Kelty Meadows Campground the road forks. Turn right on road 6S10 (The Gooseberry Flat Road) and drive for one mile. Willow Creek Wall is the 100' wall on the north side of the road just before Willow Creek.

THE BALLS

CHAPTER 4

The rumor of beautiful granite domes, unknown to all but the most inquisitive, has been a recurring theme in Southern Yosemite Climbing. No other area reflects this theme as well as The Balls. Located just three miles south of the boundary of Yosemite National Park, a good road passes directly below the row of stately granite domes. As beautiful and remote as The Balls are, logging activity still continues nearby. Some people feel that the area deserves national park or wilderness status, for indeed it was part of the Yosemite Land Grant before the realignments of the early 1900s.

Climbing history here has been the source of some confusion. The early ascents here were accomplished by Royal Robbins and his Rockcraft groups who spent several summers in The Balls during the mid-70s. Some of the routes climbed in this era were recorded in Robbin's small typewritten guide to western foothills east of Fresno or The Hinterlands as he was fond of calling it. A short bolt ladder for aid practice that dates back to this era can still be seen on a 20 foot high boulder below Boulder Garden Slab. However, bolts tended to be the exeption with chock protected climbs being the standard of the day, leaving no evidence of the ascent. During the late 70s, several groups including Tom Higgins, Bob Kamps, Cris Vandiver, and Alan Nelson were active in the area. Much of the activity was centered on the fantastic east face of Tempest Dome. Beginning in the early 1980s, Gary Fluitt along with others were active during the summers, establishing several routes on Nightwatch, The Golden Toad, No Name Ridge and Boulder Garden Slab.

From Bass Lake, it is a 45 minute drive up good roads to The Balls. From the north shore of Bass Lake, turn north on the Beasore road and follow it for 26 miles, the last 6 of which are dirt. Jones Store at Beasore Meadow has some supplies, but it may not be open in early or late season. Once you reach the 26 mile mark the domes can be easily identified on the hillside above the road. Bowler Campground is located two miles further at the eastern end of The Balls and offers outhouses but no piped in water. Bring your own water or purify the water from streams running nearby.

The climbing season here is best in high summer due to the 7500' elevation. The road is usually clear of snow by May or a bit earlier if you can crash through the early season drifts. The large south faces of most of the domes provide sunny fall climbing until winter snows close the road in late November.

Trish finds it difficult to get into last year's lycra tights.

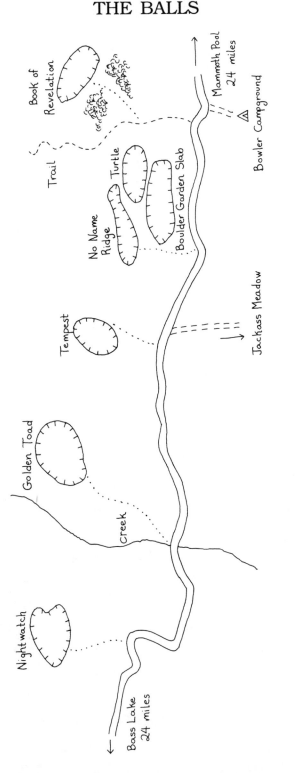

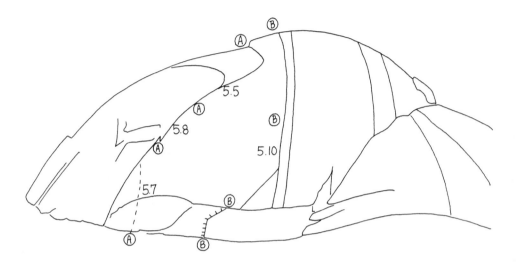

NIGHTWATCH

A Arch-A-Poko II 5.8
B Left Ski Track II 5.10

Approach Park on the Beasore Road below the dome and hike directly up the slabs to the south face. To descend, walk off to the north then work around the west side back to the road.

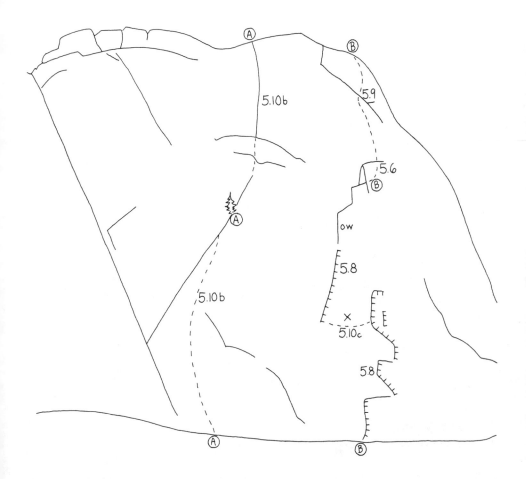

THE GOLDEN TOAD - North Face

A   Mr. Toad's Wild Ride II 5.10b
B   Adrenaline Junkies II 5.10c

Approach Park at a turnout near a creek which flows under the road. Hike up orange colored slabs right of the creek to a flat area with many boulders. The south face is directly ahead. Work left around the base of the dome to approach climbs on the west and north faces. The northeast corner of the dome provides a 4th class descent.

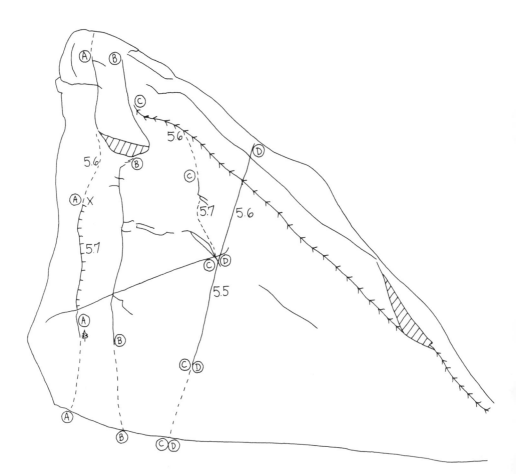

THE GOLDEN TOAD - West Face

A **Sven and Yorgie** II 5.7
B **Eye of the Toad** II 5.8
C **Revenge of King Oscar** II 5.7
D **West Face Route** II 5.6

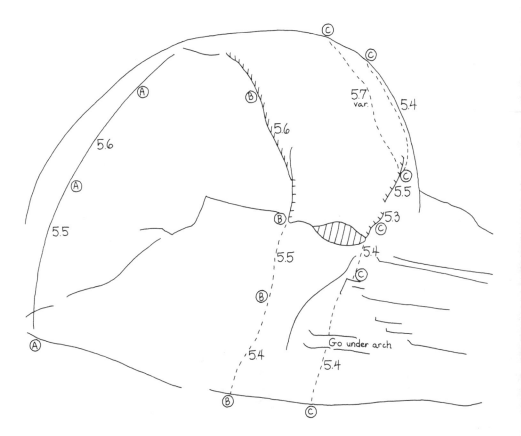

THE GOLDEN TOAD - South Face

A   **Southwest Ridge** II 5.6
B   **South Face Arch** II 5.6
C   **Eye of the Needle** II 5.5

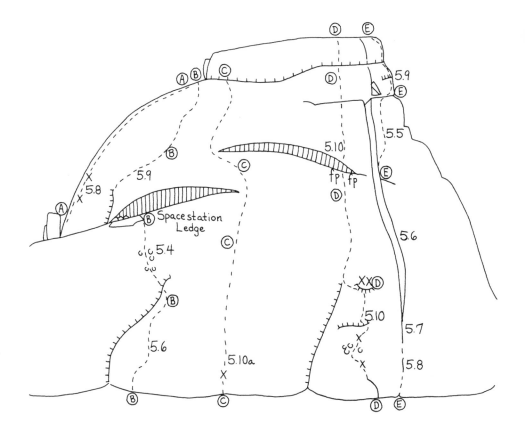

TEMPEST DOME

TEMPEST DOME - <u>East Face</u>

A Glee II 5.8   Beginning on the west side of the dome is a long ledge that crosses much of the south face. Walk up right on this ledge to a large block. From the block, climb up past two bolts for two pitches.

B Odyssey II 5.9   At the base of the south face, just left of center, is a prominent arch. Climb the face just right of this arch to its top (5.6). Climb up and left across the arch then up knobs (5.4) to Space Station Ledge. The Starship, a large, knobby block, docked on the ledge is plainly visible from below. Twenty feet left is a flake. Climb the flake and the face to its right until the wall becomes vertical. Diagonal up and right across this steep wall (5.9) until the angle eases. One more easy pitch leads to the top.

C Plate Route II 5.10a   To the right of the Odyssey arch climb a headwall past a bolt. Face climbing leads to a belay below a second headwall. Climb around this headwall and belay at the base of the third headwall. Work left around it and up the face above.

D Havana Ball II 5.10   Near the right end of the south face is a prominent black water streak with a blank face just to the left. Climb a flake through this initial headwall to a bolt. Knobs lead up to another bolt below a roof. Surmount the roof (5.10) to the right and wander up easier climbing to a double bolt belay in some bucket ledges. Traverse left to a crack then diagonal up and right to a stance 20 feet below the headwall. Climb past two fixed pins then directly over the headwall (5.10). One more pitch leads straight up to the summit.

E Miranda II 5.9   See topo.

<u>North Face</u>

Shady Lane 5.7   Climb the main dihedral on the North Face. Not much is known about these climbs.

Little Froggy 5.7   Climb the green lichen speckled wall on the North Face. Good luck!

BOULDER GARDEN SLAB

A Water Cracks
  Left 5.3
  Right 5.4
B First Lead 5.5
C Corporate Raiders II 5.7
D Big Country II 5.8
E Bare Minimum II 5.9
F Bell Bottom Blues II 5.9
G Hot Tin Roof II 5.8
H Aquarius 5.7
I Night Driver 5.6

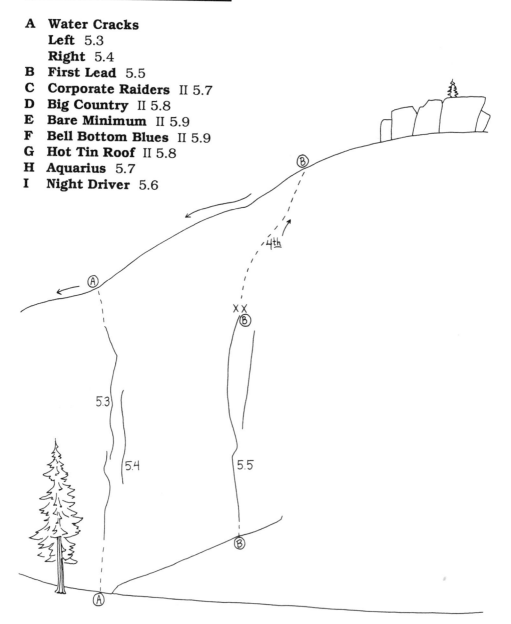

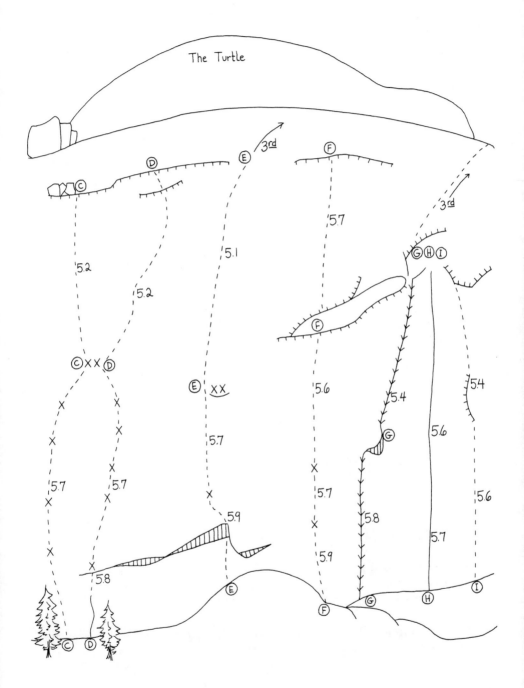

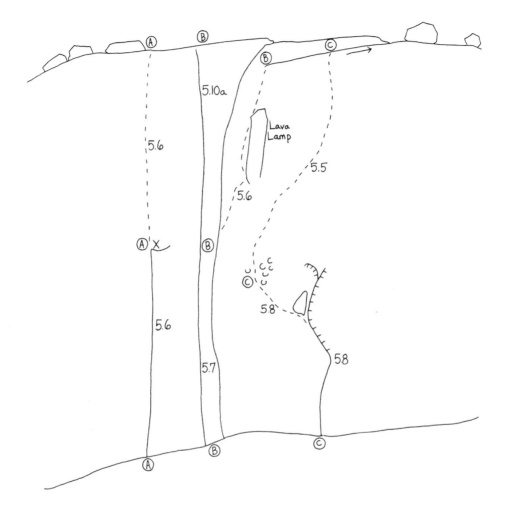

NO NAME RIDGE

A **Woodstock** II 5.6
B **Lava Lamp** II 5.10a
C **To Be Continued** II 5.8

These climbs lie on the broad 200 foot high wall up and left of Boulder Garden Slab.

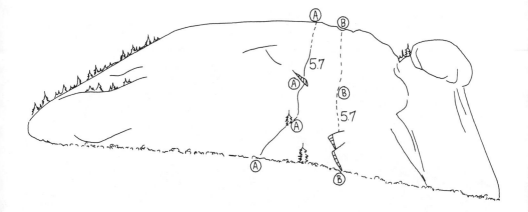

BOOK OF REVELATION

A Niki's Nimbility II 5.7
B Dave's Breakfast II 5.7

Approach Walk up the old Jackass Trail. At the lower end of the southeast face there is a faint dry wash that can be followed to the base of the rock. Although a bit obscure, this wash provides the only passage through the vicious manzanita that guards the wall.

MAMMOTH
POOL

CHAPTER 5

Mammoth Pool reservoir, 40 miles east of North Fork is the reference point for the diverse collection of domes that lie scattered along the edge of the spectacular San Joaquin River Canyon. The west face of Balloon Dome, towering 3000' above the canyon floor is easily the dominant feature when looking north from the Mile High Overlook. Across the canyon are the magnificent south faces of the Fuller Buttes which are still considered to have some of the best granite in the range. Lower down in the woods are the hidden gems of Chiquito Dome, Dissappearing Dome, and the convoluted east face of Jackass Rock. Even more obscure are the faces of Tranquility Dome and Mammoth Pool Dome which can only be identified from Mammoth Pool Reservoir on the floor of the San Joaquin River Canyon.

Technical climbers began exploring the area in the early 1970s and quickly zeroed in on the east face of the Fuller Buttes. Jerry Coe and Galen Rowell climbed the **Eagle Dihedral** IV 5.8 A2, while Fred Beckey with a variety of partners went to work on the steep **Southeast Face** IV 5.8 A2 of the Eastern Butte. Using an array of aid techniques, he finally succeeded in May of 1972 along with five other climbers who showed up to help; one jumared the entire climb. Later in the 70s several other Fuller Butte routes such as **Fear of Flying** IV 5.11c, **Zephyr** II 5.10a, and **Easy Wind** II 5.8 were put up by Steve McCabe and fellow Manx Mountaineers John Stoddard, Mary Ellen Lawerence, and Gerri Dayharsh. The Manx Mountaineers were responsible for several fine routes in the area including the striking **Memphis Blues** IV 5.11a on Dissappearing Dome. On an early attempt of this route they became hopelessly disoriented on the return hike to the car through the thick logging slash. The name Dissappearing Dome was coined to commemorate their adventure. They persevered however, and returned to climb several routes both at Mammoth Pool and on Shuteye Ridge. Another hardworking combination during the late 70s and early 80s was the trio of Simon King, Fremont Brainbridge, and Conrad Van Bruggen. In addition to explorations of West Fuller Butte and Jackass Rock, the trio discovered and climbed three fine routes on Tranquility Dome, a beautiful 700' face hidden high up on the wall of the San Joaquin River Canyon just below the Mile High Overlook. Another focus of their attention was the south face of nearby Chiquito Dome on which they climbed several routes. First climbed in 1975 by Jack Delk and Guy McClure, this elegant dome has been the site of continued activity throughout the 80s. Tom Higgins and Cris Vandiver established their classic **Elegant Inclinations** III 5.11a in 1980 and returned three years later to climb the runout **Sahib** III 5.10b. More recently, in 1986, Vaino Kodas, Patrick Paul, and Greg Vernon have been active at Chiquito Dome, putting up several new routes.

The Minarets Road (Rd. 4S00) leads from North Fork 40 miles to Mammoth Pool Reservoir. The approach information for each of the domes in the area uses this road as a reference. Several campgrounds are located in close proximity to the climbing areas. Soda Springs Campground at 4300' is the best basecamp for climbing at Chiquito Dome. Camping is free but there is no piped in water. Several campgrounds near Mammoth Pool Reservoir provide a good base for Mammoth Pool Dome and Tranquility Dome. There is also good camping at the Squaw Dome trailhead and the Fuller Buttes trailhead (bring your own water). Little Jackass Campground at 4900' is 6 miles south of Jackass Rock and Fuller Buttes. It is a small primitive campground with 6 sites but it does have a creek running nearby.

While the lower elevation domes such as Mammoth Pool Dome can be climbed year round, the access along the Minarets Road is the limiting factor for the climbing season. The road reaches an elevation of 5600' near Mile High Curve and climbs to 6800' near Squaw Dome. In the past the road was commonly locked near Fish Creek Camp during the winter season regardless of the road conditions. Recently, a new open gate policy is being tested, allowing for early access in low snow conditions. On the other hand, access to Mammoth Pool Reservoir continues to be restricted from May 1 to June 16 for deer migration across Mammoth Pool. The gate is locked at the Mammoth Pool Campground 5 miles short of Mammoth Pool Dome and Tranquility Dome. Mountain bikes are permitted in the area however, providing easy access on good dirt roads. For current road and campground information for the Mammoth Pool area call the Minarets Ranger Station at (209) 877-2218.

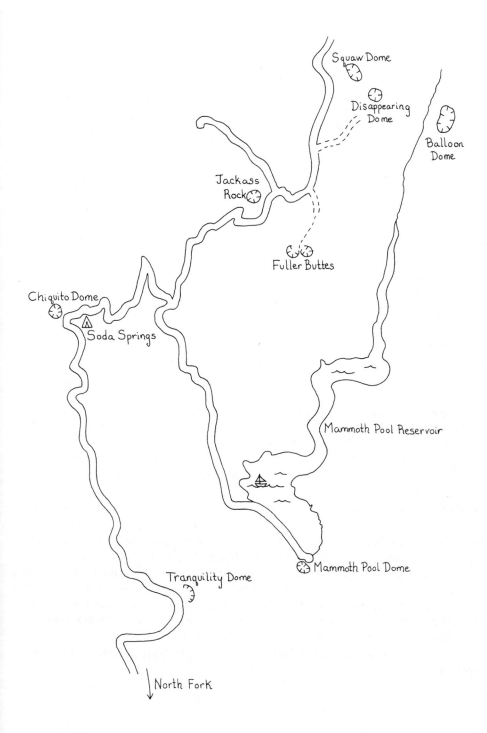

Squaw Dome

Disappearing Dome

Balloon Dome

Jackass Rock

Fuller Buttes

Chiquito Dome

Soda Springs

Mammoth Pool Reservoir

Tranquility Dome

Mammoth Pool Dome

North Fork

<u>Approach</u>

Without a doubt, the crux of any Balloon Dome route is the approach. There are two choices.

West Side - From McCreary Meadow, north of Mammoth Pool on the Minarets Road, take the trail to Cassidy Meadow. Follow the trail into the canyon, 2200 feet below to the Cassidy Crossing, which can be difficult to ford during spring runoff. Once back up to the canyon rim, head south, cross country to Balloon Dome. Plan on a full day for this 8 mile stroll.

East Side - Take Highway 168 from Fresno to Huntington Lake, 67 miles distant. Follow signs over Kaiser Pass to Lake Edison. From the lake dirt roads lead west four miles to Onion Spring Meadow. Walk up the dirt road to Fawn Meadow, Bear Meadow then Cassidy Meadow, 10 miles distant. Just before Cassidy Meadow cut back south to Balloon Dome. Even though this approach is longer, it has less elevation gain than the west side approach, and is preferred during the spring runoff. Wilderness permits are required to enter the wilderness at Lake Edison. Permits are issued at the Pineridge Ranger Station in Shaver Lake and the High Sierra Ranger Station near Mono Hot Springs. The Kaiser Pass road is usually open May through November. Check with Pineridge Ranger Station for current road conditions. The phone number is 209-841-3311.

BALLOON DOME

Beckey Route IV 5.8 A3   A large pillar which resembles The Lost Arrow leans up against the northeast face of the dome. Climb steep slabs and cracks up the left side of this formation for five pitches to its top. Rappel 50 feet into the notch behind it, then pendulum right to a thin aid crack. Aid up this crack for a pitch then continue up on easier friction to the summit.

Boku-Muru III 5.9   Just left of the pillar of the Beckey route is a smooth wall broken only by a dike which leads up and left. Climb two pitches to the base of the dike. Follow the dike for seven more pitches to the summit. Nine bolts were placed.

East Face III 5.9   This route follows the first chimney system to the left of Boku-Muru. Climb the chimney for two pitches. Traverse out right on the face to a crack which is followed for five more pitches to the summit. Bring many small wired nuts for this crack.

West Face IV 5.9 A3   A prominent left-facing open book lies in the center of the west face overlooking the San Joaquin River. Begin on the large ledge that splits the west face. Seven pitches, about half aid, lead to the summit.

Southeast Face Class 3   Friction slabs on the left side of the east face provide a class 3 dscent from the summit.

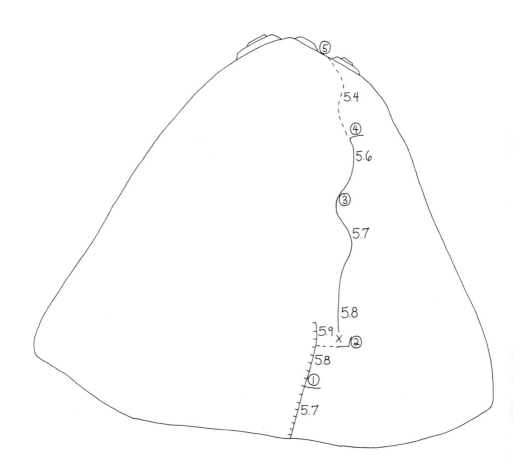

SQUAW DOME - North Face

Snake Crack II 5.9
pro: tiny to 2.5"

SQUAW DOME - West Face

A   West Book II 5.6
Begin in the large, right facing book which dominates the west face of Squaw
Dome. Climb up for two pitches of 5.6 to a point where the book steepens.
Traverse right and up 5.6 face climbing for one more pitch to the unroping
spot.

Approach
Squaw Dome can be identified as northernmost of three connected domes
just south of McCreary Meadow. The Minarets Road passes within a mile of
the dome, providing reasonable access. To approach the west face, drive
about one half mile past (north of) the Graveyard Meadow turnoff to a posted
15 MPH corner. A small wooden sign labeled "French Trail 1/4 Mile" marks
a road which leads northeast toward Squaw Dome. Drive down this road 1/
4 mile to a good campsite in an open sandy area with a fire ring. Park here
and hike up the slope to the base of the west face. To approach **Snake Crack**,
either work north, along the brushy base of the face, or approach directly
through the woods from the vicinity of McCreary Meadow.

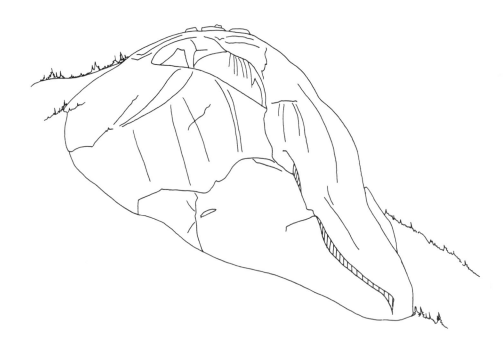

DISSAPPEARING DOME

Dissappearing Dome, invisible from many viewpoints, can be identified as point 7480, located 0.75 mile southeast of Squaw Dome.   To reach Dissappearing Dome, drive north on the Minarets Road, four miles past Jackass Rock. A dirt road on the right (east side of the road) is marked by a sign for the South Fork Trailhead. Follow signs for 1.5 miles to the trailhead, avoiding the left road forks which lead to recent logging areas. From the vicinity of the trailhead, Dissappearing Dome will be seen to the north, overlooking the San Joaquin River Canyon. Continue driving north, along the canyon rim, past the South Fork Trailhead. Within 3/4 mile the road dissappears in logging slash just south of the dome. Park here and work down along the margin of the east face to the start of the climbs. Allow 30 minutes for the approach, depending on how far you are able to drive. To descend, walk off through the brush on the south slope of the dome to the logging area. Be warned: the name Dissappearing Dome originated when the first ascent party became hopelessly lost trying to find their way back from the dome after an early attempt on the face.

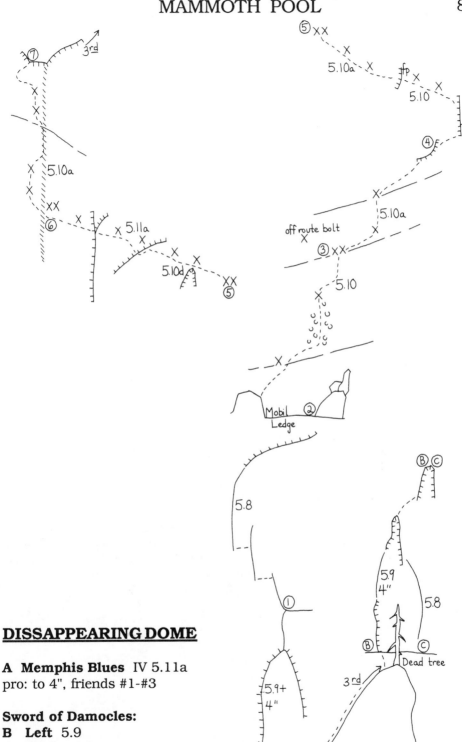

DISSAPPEARING DOME

A Memphis Blues IV 5.11a
pro: to 4", friends #1-#3

Sword of Damocles:
B   Left 5.9
C   Right 5.8

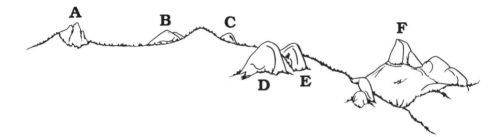

MAMMOTH POOL PANORAMA

A Jackass Rock
B Squaw Dome
C Dissappearing Dome
D West Fuller Butte
E East Fuller Butte
F Balloon Dome

From the Mile High Overlook, on the Minarets / Mammoth Pool road, the domes are easily identified. This is the view to the north. The view to the east of the Shuteye Ridge domes as well as Chiquito Dome can be found on page 112-113 and 128 in the Shuteye Ridge chapter.

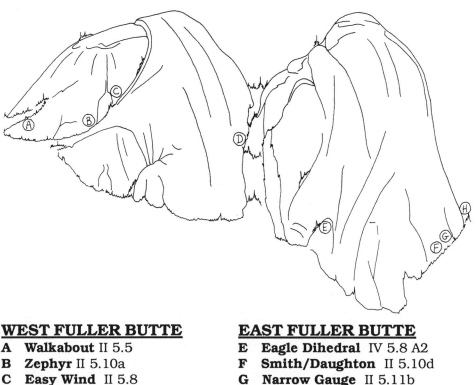

WEST FULLER BUTTE

A   **Walkabout** II 5.5
B   **Zephyr** II 5.10a
C   **Easy Wind** II 5.8
D   **East Face** III 5.9 A1

EAST FULLER BUTTE

E   **Eagle Dihedral** IV 5.8 A2
F   **Smith/Daughton** II 5.10d
G   **Narrow Gauge** II 5.11b
H   **Southwest Face** IV 5.8 A2

Approach
Although Fuller Buttes have been approached from faint logging tracks on
the south, the easiest approach is from the north along an old logging road
which ends on a wooded bench just north of Fuller Buttes. To find this
particular logging road, drive north on the Minarets Road to a point one mile
past (northeast) Jackass rock. Just as the road gains its high point and
turns away from Fuller Buttes, turn right (south) onto a paved road which
soon turns to dirt. Continue on this road for almost one half mile to a hairpin
corner. A blocked off road can be seen climbing up the hillside to the right.
Park here and walk along this road for one half mile to small saddle. At this
point another logging track crosses our path and climbs up the hill to the left
(east) and ends atop a small knoll. Don't take this dead end, but continue
straight ahead on the faint road for one more mile to the top of the Buttes.
For climbs on the East Face of the East Butte work east, down the margin
of the East Face. Climbs on the south faces of both Buttes can be reached
by descending the gully between the Buttes. It is interesting to note that
some individuals in four-wheel-drive vehicles have managed to bypass the
road block at the hairpin turn, making the walk in substantially shorter.
Mountain bikes can also serve this same purpose, with a little less
environmental impact.

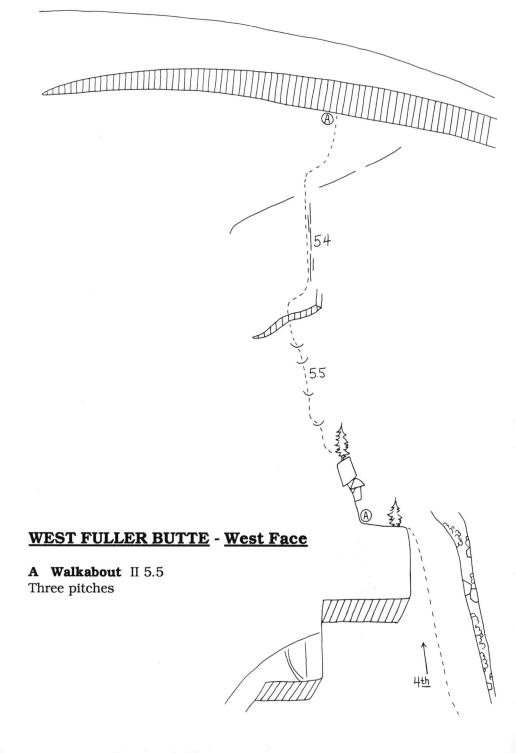

WEST FULLER BUTTE - West Face

A **Walkabout** II 5.5
Three pitches

WEST FULLER BUTTE - South Face

A Zephyr II 5.10a
pro: tiny to 3.5", #4 friend

B Easy Wind II 5.8
pro: tiny to 3.5"

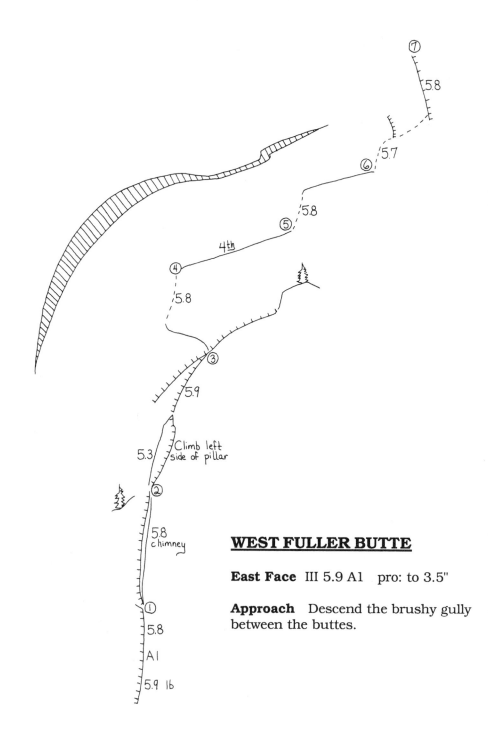

7

5.8

5.7

6

5.8

5

4th

4

5.8

5.9

3

5.3

Climb left
side of pillar

2

5.8
chimney

1

5.8

A1

5.9 1b

WEST FULLER BUTTE

East Face   III 5.9 A1   pro: to 3.5"

Approach   Descend the brushy gully
between the buttes.

EAST FULLER BUTTE

SOUTH FACE

Eagle Dihedral IV 5.9 A3
The route takes on the obvious, left leaning dihedral on the southwest face of the dome. Begin in the gully between the Buttes and walk right, out a ramp onto the face to the start of the dihedral. Climb the dihedral for three pitches to a tricky ceiling. On the first ascent the climbers aided to the lip of the roof then executed a 15 foot nut throw in order to surmount the roof. Above the roof, easier cracks, chimneys, and a few easier overhangs lead to a long ledge just below the summit. Walk the ledge around the corner to an easy chimney that leads to the summit slabs. It was on the first ascent that the climbers, rounding this corner, almost collided with an eagle coming in to land on the ledge, hence the name.

EAST FACE

Southeast Face IV 5.8 A2
Near the longest portion of the Southeast face, a huge hourglass shaped flake will be seen attached to the upper half of the wall. The route gains the right side of this hourglass via a bolt ladder from a large flake which rests against the base of the wall, 200' below. Begin the climb in a short, awkward chimney on the right side of this flake to a third class ledge. From the high point of the ledge, a long bolt ladder with many bat-hook holes leads to the beginning of the crack system above. Climb free up the beautiful open book until the crack in the dihedral narrows. Aid up the steep crack until the angle eases. At this point it is possible to lasso a horn-shaped flake to the left and climb the face left of the crack. Two more fifth class pitches lead to the summit. Bring protection to 4" as well as 3/16" bat-hooks.

Songs to a Morning Star III 5.10
Begin uphill, to the right of the **Southeast Face Route** and **Fear of Flying**. The route begins in cracks 20' right of a large curving dihedral. The crux is a 5.10 lieback under a prominent arch on the second pitch. Above, climb easy moves past a small pine tree, then face climbing leads up and left to a belay at a large flake. The next pitch climbs up and right to a white dike (5.6 but unprotected) which leads to a spacious, sickle-shaped ledge. Three more pitches lead up and around the left side of the eastern summit block.

White Dike II 5.9
Begin up and right of **Songs to a Morning Star** on a white dike that spans the polished granite wall. The four pitch climb has bolt belays as well as several protection bolts on long runouts.

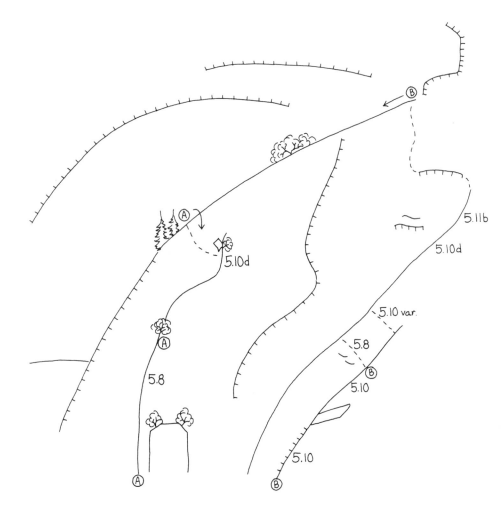

EAST FULLER BUTTE - East Face

A Smith/Daughton II 5.10d
B Narrow Guage II 5.11b
pro: RPs, many tiny nuts,
double set of friends #1-#3

Approach Hike down along the base of the east face past several routes. These climbs are at the extreme south end of the east face, downhill and left of the prominent hourglass flake that marks Fred Beckey's Southeast Face route.

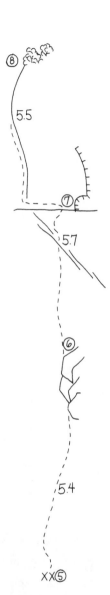

XX ⑤

5.5

↑
165'
↓

⑧

5.5

④ sb

5.7

⑦

5.7

③

5.9

5.10a

5.10c

② sb

5.10b

X   X

X

①

5.10

5.11c

X

X

⑥

5.4

XX⑤

EAST FULLER BUTTE
- East Face

Fear of Flying III 5.11c

JACKASS ROCK

A **Vicious** II 5.9
B **Don't Look Back** II 5.8
C **Apple Ranch** II 5.6
D **Nick Bottom** 5.6
E **Puck** II 5.9+

The climbs are found on the broad east face of Jackass Rock. Vicious and Don't Look Back are located under the right end of a long ceiling. A short distance right is a prominent 100 foot wide alcove. Apple Ranch climbs the left side of this alcove while Nick Bottom and Puck follow its right. Park off the road below the east face and hike up brushy slopes for 10-15 minutes to reach the base of the rock.

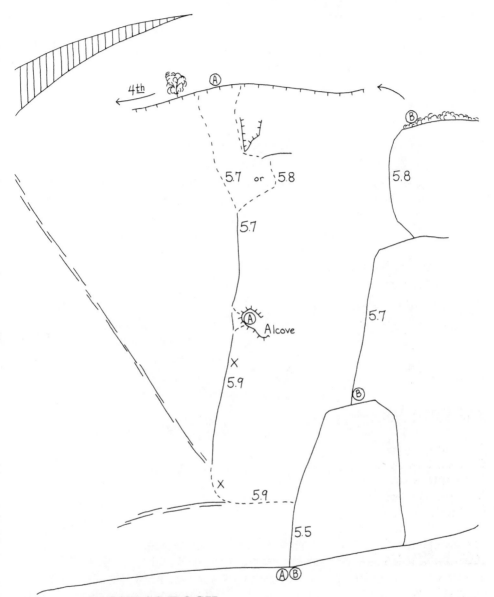

JACKASS ROCK

A Vicious II 5.9
Place a nut high to protect the initial 5.9 dike traverse.

B Don't Look Back II 5.8

JACKASS ROCK

A   Nick Bottom 5.6
B   Puck II 5.9+
Rappel or continue for 2 more easy pitches

Apple Ranch II 5.6   Begin in a deep, black chimney 100 ft. down and left of Nick Bottom. Climb up this chimney (5.6) to a good belay ledge. Above the ledge, and slightly right of the prominent right facing corner, 3 pitches lead up flakes and cracks to the unroping spot. Walk right (north) and descend easier slabs and gullies.

LETTERS TO PAUL

Betrayed 5.10a
Rappel down back. Beware of bad bolts.

Approach This area is located 1.5 miles west of Jackass Rock on the Mammoth Pool Road. The rocks are just off the road to the north.

MAMMOTH POOL DOME

A   That Little Strapless Number III 5.10c
pro: include #0.5 tri-cam

B   Mammoth Pool Madness A2
Climb the obvious roof crack

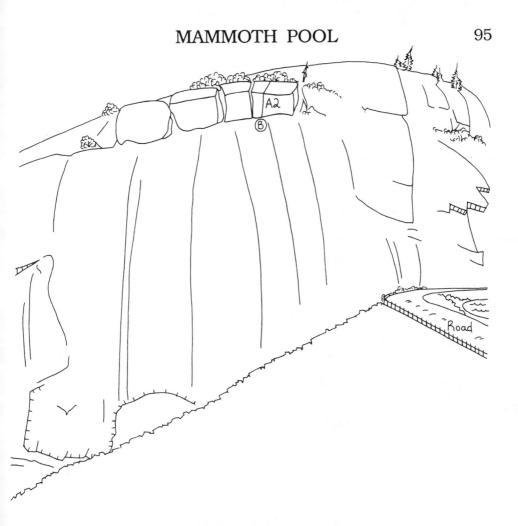

<u>MAMMOTH POOL DOME</u>

Mammoth Pool Dome (elevation 3639) is located between the spillway and dam at the south end of Mammoth Pool Reservoir. A good gravel road leads to within a few feet of the east face. **That Little Strapless Number** begins near the bottom of the dam at the second of three wooden ramps. Begin climbing from the silver #11 marker which has been glued to the base of the wall by construction crews.

Several campgrounds as well as a small store and gas station are located along the west shore of the lake. With the low elevation of the lake, summer temperatures often force mid-day swim breaks in the typical climbing day. **NOTE**: the gate near the Mammoth Pool Campground is locked from May 1 to June 16 to allow deer migration across Mammoth Pool. This restriction affects the approach for both Mammoth Pool Dome and Tranquility Dome. While vehicles are prohibited, mountain bikes are legal on the road which leads the last three miles to the spillway.

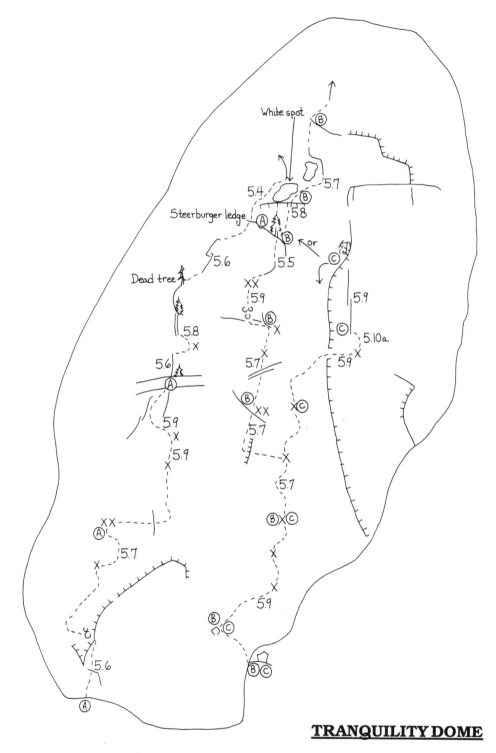

White spot

B

5.7

5.4

B

5.8

Steerburger ledge

A

B

or

C

5.6

5.5

Dead tree

XX

5.9

5.9

B

X

5.8

X

5.7

C

5.10a

5.6

A

5.9

B

5.9

X

XX

X C

5.9

X

5.7

5.7

A

XX

B X C

5.7

X

5.7

X

B C

5.9

B C

5.6

B C

A

TRANQUILITY DOME

TRANQUILITY DOME

A **Visions** III 5.9
B **Suicide Claim** III 5.9
C **Blind Ambition** III 5.10a

Tranquility Dome is the 700 foot gray face located high on the canyon wall, west of the San Joaquin River, just below Mile High Curve on the Mammoth Pool Road. On the Shuteye Peak topo map Tranquility Dome can be identified as the small white oval 0.2 mile north of the words Mile High Curve. The dome is plainly visible from below at Mammoth Pool Reservoir.

Approach Follow the Mammoth Pool Road around the reservoir and down toward the dam. About 3/4 mile before the dam a rough dirt road leads right (south) down towards the river. Park at the end of this road at a large sand embankment, and hike due west to the base of the rock. **NOTE**: The gate near the entrance to the Mammoth Pool Campground is locked from May 1 to June 15 to allow deer migration across Mammoth Pool. This closure results in a 4-5 mile hike to get to the approach trailhead. While vehicles are prohibited during deer migration, mountain bikes are legal, providing a faster and more pleasant approach to the trailhead. An alternate approach begins from the Mammoth Pool Road at the Mile High Overlook. Rappel down the face to the start of the climbs. This approach is not very obvious from above. Scout out the dome thouroughly from below before attempting to approach it from above.

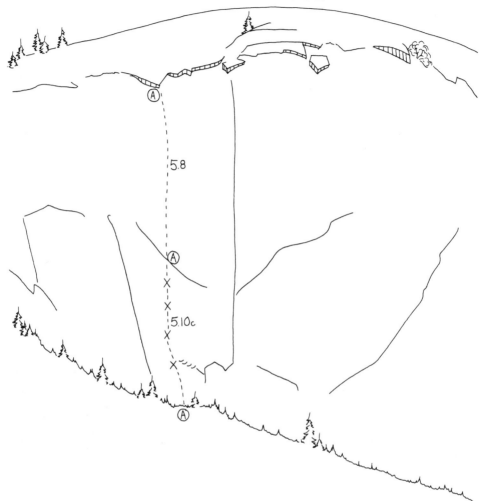

CHIQUITO DOME

A   **August Knights** II 5.10c
B   **Sahib** III 5.10b
C   **Elegance** III 5.11a
D   **KOPA** 5.11a

Approach
The southeast face of Chiquito Dome is easily seen from the Mammoth Pool Road, 1/2 mile west of Soda Springs Campground. From the point where the road passes close to the dome, park at a turnout and hike west, up the forested slope to the base of the southeast face. Allow 20-30 minutes for the approach.

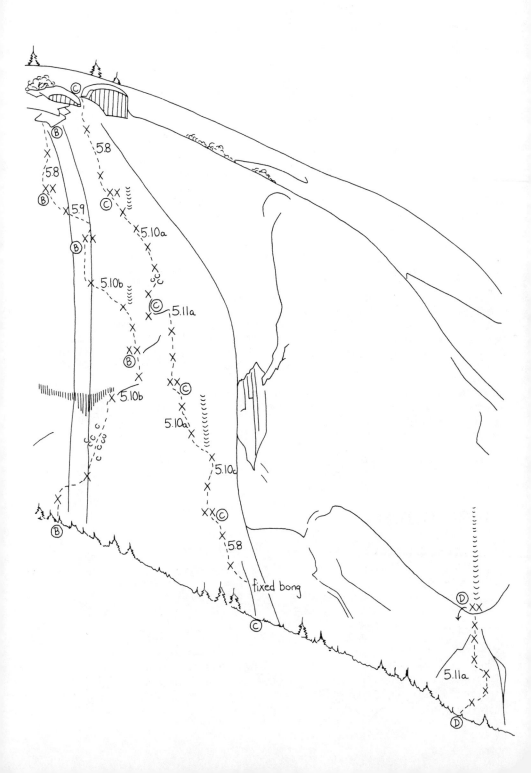

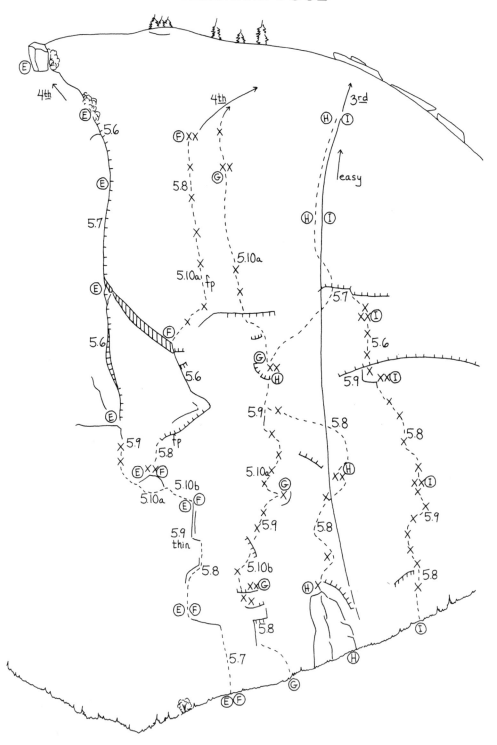

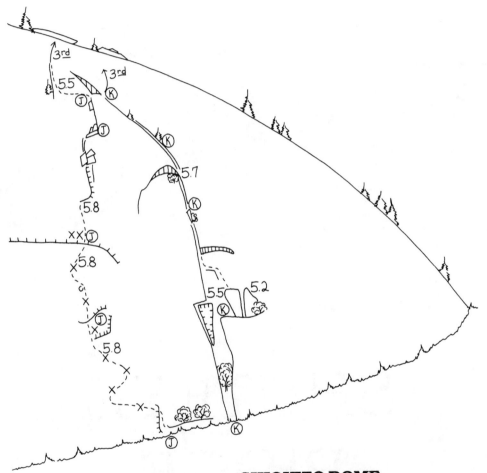

CHIQUITO DOME

E	**South Chimney**	III 5.10b
F	**Top Gun**	III 5.10b
G	**Liberty**	III 5.10b
H	**Archline**	III 5.9
I	**The Acolyte**	II 5.9
J	**Jigsaw Puzzle**	II 5.8
K	**Cheeseburger in Paradise**	II 5.7

SHUTEYE
RIDGE

CHAPTER 6

The vast sea of rock surrounding Shuteye Ridge provides the greatest amount of climbing possibilities in the Southern Yosemite area. This is wilderness climbing at its finest. Furthermore, the backcountry flavor is maintained by dirt roads and sometimes hour long, brush filled approach hikes which effectively guard the rock from overcrowding. The even distribution of domes around Shuteye Ridge, effectively disperses climbers throughout the area.

The climbing history on Shuteye Ridge begins with Fred Beckey's 1972 ascent of the **East Face** of the South Eagle Beak. Together with Hooman Aprin, he characteristically spotted the most prominent route on the face and climbed it. The next year Royal Robbins began exploring the area with his Rockcraft school. Over the next few years they established several routes on the Queens Throne, Minerva Dome, and The Bastion. However, many of the Rockcraft School's routes were never recorded. With so much rock, they just wandered the area, climbing anything that looked good, often using the recently introduced nuts to provide clean protection. During this time period, local Jack Delk began his exploration of the "Eagle Domes" on the east flank of Shuteye Ridge. His continuing efforts have been rewarded by many fine routes, some up to 1000 feet high on the east faces of these domes. During the early 1980's the trio of Simon King, Fremont Brainbridge, and Conrad Van Bruggen were active in the Eagle Beaks area, putting up routes such as **Thunder Road** III 5.9, **Beak Job** II 5.8 and **Beagle Creeks** II 5.8. Rock Creek Wall was discovered and developed during this time as well. And finally, Steve McCabe and the Manx Mountaineers braved the brush once again to climb **The Big Sleep** III 5.9 and the demanding **Voodoo Child** 5.10d on The Big Sleep Dome just west of Shuteye Pass.

With the wide distribution of domes on Shuteye Ridge, many different approaches present themselves. Almost all trailheads can be reached within

45 minutes to 1 hour from North Fork. In this chapter, specific approaches as well as campgrounds will be listed with the dome or in some cases, in the area overview. The Forest Service dispersed camping policy makes it possible to camp near several of the climbing areas in this region. The environment in the upper portions of Shuteye Ridge is as fragile as it is beautiful. It is essential to practice low impact camping, as well as climbing. If we all make an effort now to prevent litter and pollution, the area will remain pristine for many years to come.

Most of the domes on Shuteye Ridge range from 7000' to 8000'. Bright summer days are perfect for climbing here while the lower elevations simmer in the vicious summer heat. The climbing season typically begins in May, as soon as the roads become snow free. The Shuteye Peak Lookout Road is usually open by mid-June, but you can get as far as the Queens Throne several weeks earlier. The cool, clear days of fall climbing usually last into November until winter snows make the roads impassable.

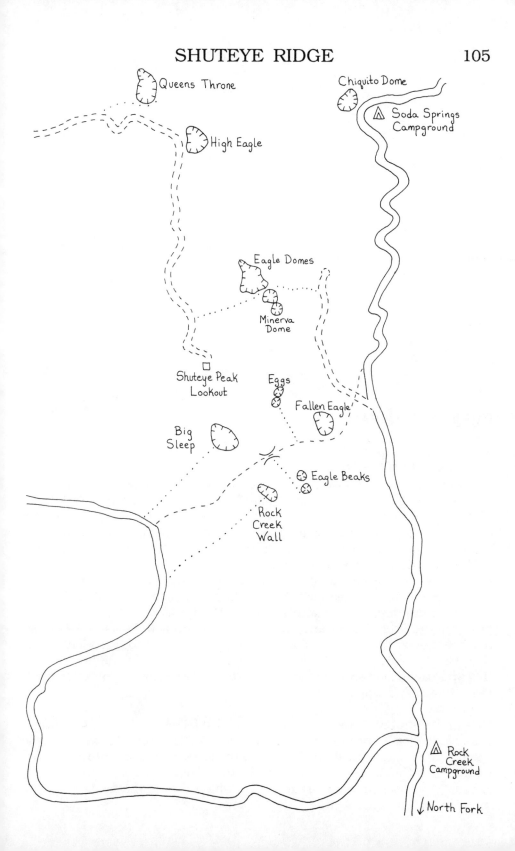

Queens Throne

Chiquito Dome

Soda Springs
Campground

High Eagle

Eagle Domes

Minerva
Dome

Shuteye Peak
Lookout

Eggs

Fallen Eagle

Big
Sleep

Eagle Beaks

Rock
Creek
Wall

Rock
Creek
Campground

↓ North Fork

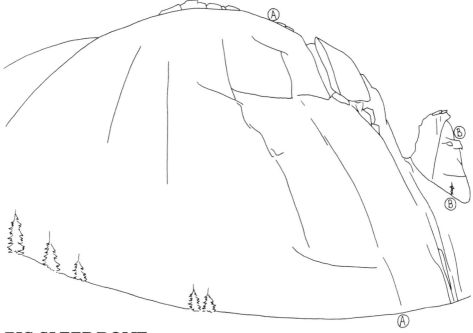

BIG SLEEP DOME

A   The Big Sleep III 5.9
B   Voodoo Child 5.10d

To reach The Big Sleep Dome, begin at the Shuteye Pass Trailhead on the west side of Shuteye Ridge, near Haskell Meadow. From North Fork there are two ways to drive to the trailhead: **A** One mile east of North Fork turn left onto the Cascadel road which soon becomes road 8S09. Follow this road north past the Whiskey Falls Campground turnoff. Continue to the junction of the Browns Meadow road (7S07) 14 miles from North Fork. At this junction, go straight ahead on the Rock Creek Road (7S02) for one mile to the Shuteye Pass Trailhead which is on the left (east) side of the road. Total distance from North Fork via this route is 15 miles. **B** The alternate route begins at the Rock Creek Campground on the Mammoth Pool Road 27 miles northeast of North Fork. One mile past the campground, turn left on the Rock Creek Road (7S02). Drive 7 miles to the Shuteye Pass Trailhead. While this approach is longer (35 miles from North Fork) it does offer better roads than the Cascadel approach.

Approach

Park at the Shuteye Pass Trailhead. Instead of following the trail to Shuteye Pass, hike north through the woods toward Big Sleep Dome, 1/2 mile distant. Just before the dome is reached the forest opens out into a large flat granite slab the size of a football field. Big Sleep Dome is visible directly ahead. Approach it via a brushy gully which drains the face. Allow 30 minutes for this approach.

BIG SLEEP DOME

The Big Sleep III 5.9
most pitches 165'-170'
pro: nuts tiny to 3"
    friends #1-#3

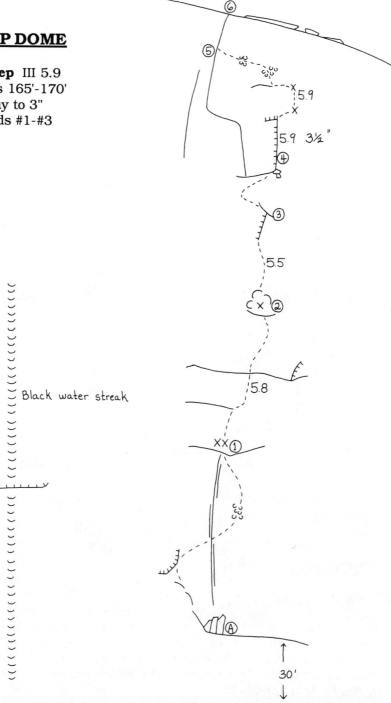

Black water streak

5.9

5.9 3½ "

5.5

5.8

30'

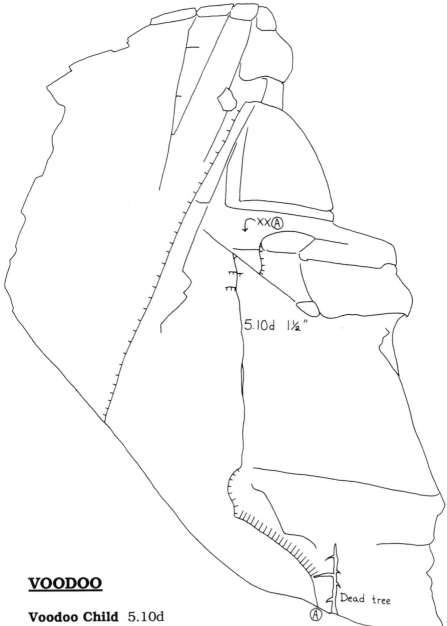

5.10d 1½"

Dead tree

VOODOO

Voodoo Child 5.10d
pro: to 3", sm. friends to #3

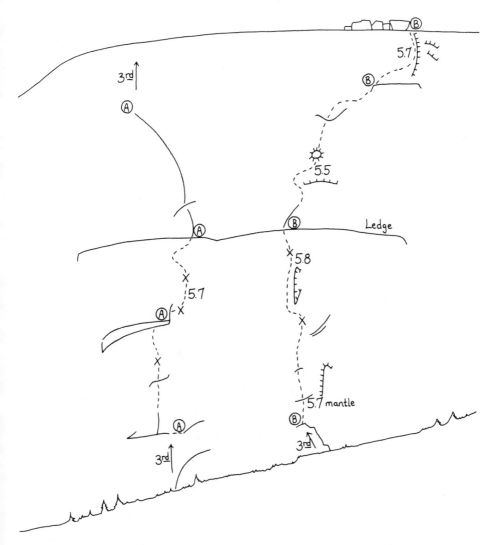

ROCK CREEK WALL

A   Walk We Crawl II 5.7
B   Soft Shoe Shuffle II 5.8

On the Mammoth Pool Road 1 mile north of the Rock Creek Campground turn west onto the Haskell Meadow Road (road 7S02). Follow this road 4 miles to Haskell Meadow. Rock Creek Wall can be identified as the obvious short wall rising to the east. Approach diagonally to the northeast through the brush. Allow 20 minutes for the approach.

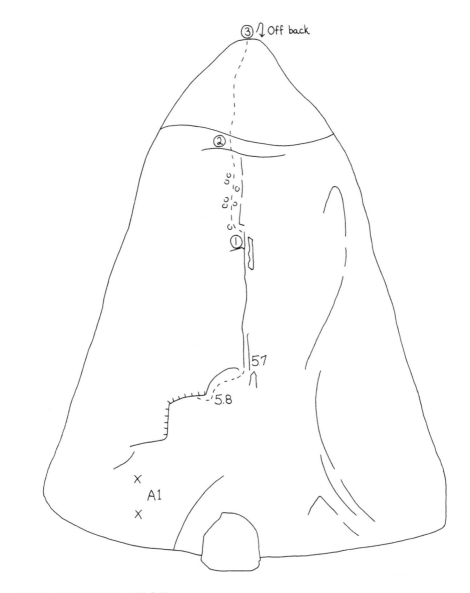

THE INCINERATOR

Routa de Fruta II 5.8 A1

Approach   From Haskell Meadow, The Incinerator can be identified as a tower high on the mountanside above Rock Creek Wall. An approach can be made by climbing Rock Creek Wall then walking east for 10 minutes to the base of the dome. An alternate approach can be made directly from the road through thick brush and boulders.

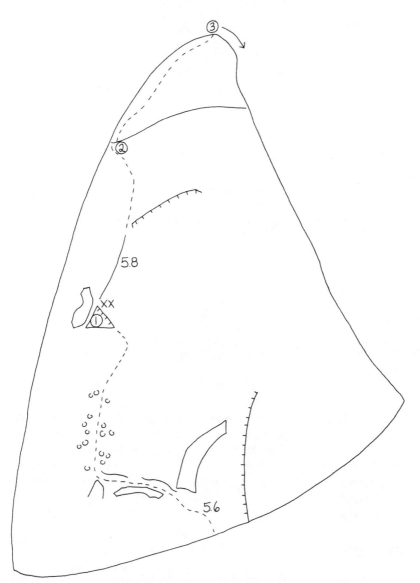

THE INCINERATOR

Stun 'Em With Science II 5.8
This climb begins up and right of Routa de Fruita.

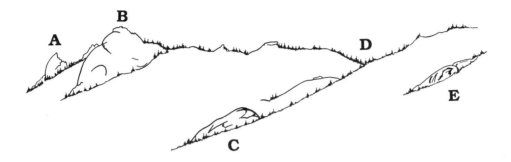

SHUTEYE RIDGE - SOUTHEAST SLOPE

A   South Eagle Beak
B   North Eagle Beak
C   Fallen Eagle Dome
D   Shuteye Pass
E   The Eggs
F   Minerva Dome
G   Red Eagle Dome
H   Gray Eagle Dome
I   The Bastion

Driving north along the Minarets Road (Rd. 4S81), 30 miles from North Fork, the numerous domes of Shuteye Ridge come into view on the hillside to the west. The Mile High Lookout, 33 miles from North Fork provides a good viewpoint for Shuteye Ridge domes as well as for the domes in the Mammoth Pool area. Another good vantage point can be found 2 miles past Soda Springs Campground (43 miles from North Fork). The panorama is drawn from this viewpoint.

Campgrounds

Rock Creek Campground - 27 miles from North Fork. There is a $5.00 per day fee to camp here. The campground has 18 campsites with piped in water. Rock Creek is a good base for climbs on either side of Chiquito Ridge. The Big Sleep and Rock Creek Wall are reached by the Rock Creek Road, while the Eagle Domes are reached by a short drive up the Minarets road to the north.

Soda Springs Campground - 41 miles from North Fork. Camping is free, but there is no piped in water. Either bring your own supply or purify water from the nearby creek. There are 18 campsites. Chiquito Dome is within easy walking distance of the campground.

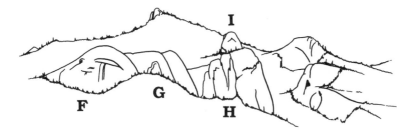

Approaches

Eagle Beaks - While the Eagle Beaks can be approached from the Minarets road on the east side, the best approach is from the west, hiking southeast from Shuteye Pass. The Eagle Beaks Overview on page 114 provides the approach description.

Fallen Eagle / The Eggs - From a point 4 miles south of Soda Springs Campground, a small sign marks the trail to Shuteye Pass. A 1/2 hour hike up this trail leads to Fallen Eagle Dome. To approach the Eggs, continue up the trail for another 1/2 mile, then strike out up the ridge that leads to The Eggs. Allow an hour from the road to reach The Eggs.

Minerva Dome / Red and Gray Eagle Domes - On the Minarets Road, one half mile south of the Shuteye Pass trail, turn left (west) on an unsigned dirt road. This road leads up and north, passing below the Eagle Domes. Follow the road for 1.5 miles to its high point. Leave the road here and strike out up the ridge toward Minerva Dome. For Red Eagle Dome and Gray Eagle Dome, work up and north, skirting the heavy brush and rough terrain as much as possible. Allow 1-1 1/2 hours for this approach, depending on how far up the dirt road you can drive.
An alternate approach with less hiking can be made from the lookout on Shuteye Peak. Park at the lookout and follow a set of electrical wires due north for 10 minutes. The Eagle Domes can be seen a short distance below. To get to the base of the domes, either scramble down the class 4 gully (Fernwood Alley) between Minerva Dome and Red Eagle Dome, or make two double rope rappels down the face of Red Eagle Dome. Begin at a tree with rappel slings just south of Triple Dihedral. Rappel to the top of the Breast Feather where another double rope rappel leads to the ground. This rappel route is also the descent for routes ending on top of the Eagle Domes.

EAGLE BEAKS

SOUTH EAGLE BEAK
A   **East Face** II 5.8 A1
B   **Beagle Creeks** II 5.8
     Opening Farewell II 5.5
     Five Years II 5.7
     (around corner on the southwest face)

NORTH EAGLE BEAK
C   **Thunder Road** III 5.9
D   **Beak Job** II 5.8

Approach
Although approaches can be made from the Mammoth Pool Road on the east side, the easiest approach is made via Shuteye Pass from the west. Park at the Shuteye Pass Trail and hike up the rough road which soon turns north and becomes a trail. After approximately 1 mile the trail reaches Shuteye Pass. Strike out east, down the ridge staying close to the crest until it is possible to work down and east to the base of the North Eagle Beak climbs. To reach climbs on the SW face of the South Eagle Beak, work down and west from the top of the ridge to the start of the prominent dihedral of Beagle Creeks. Opening Farewell and Five Years are located a few hundred feet right of Beagle Creeks. Allow 1 hour for the approach.

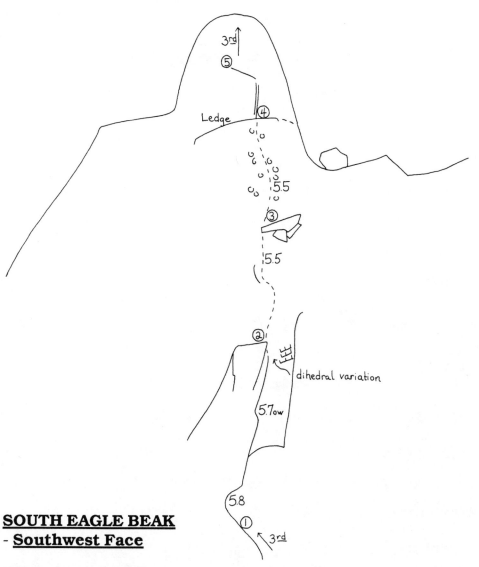

SOUTH EAGLE BEAK
- Southwest Face

Beagle Creeks II 5.8
This climb begins in the major dihedral on the southwest face.

(not illustrated)
Opening Farewell II 5.5
Climb two pitches up the obvious large water groove a few hundred feet right of Beagle Creeks. Tie off knobs for protection.

Five Years II 5.7
Begin atop a pillar to the right of Opening Farewell. Climb two pitches up the knobby face.

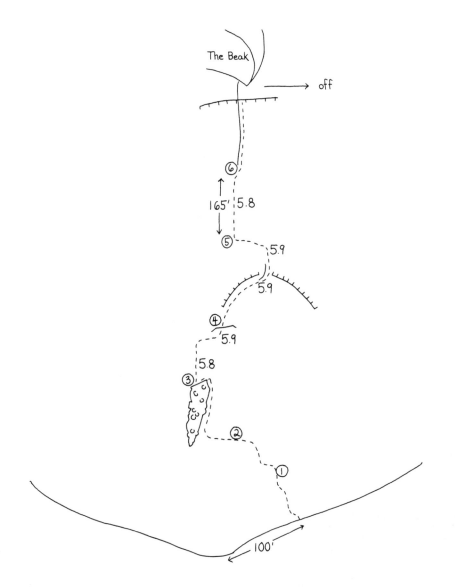

NORTH EAGLE BEAK

Thunder Road III 5.9
Begin 100' up and right of the low point of the east face apron.

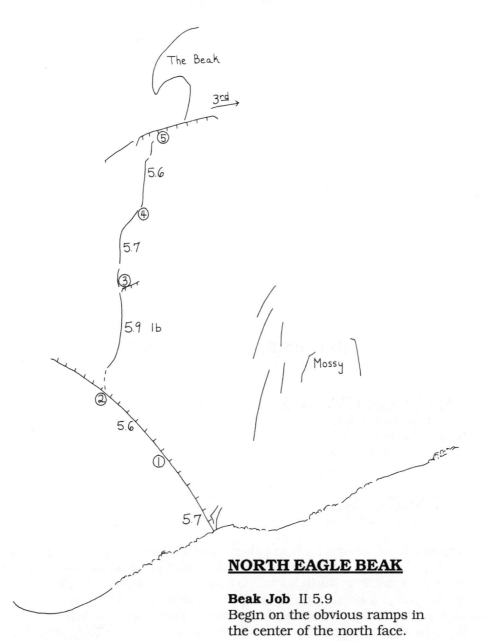

The Beak

3rd →

⑤

5.6

④

5.7

③

5.9 1b

②

5.6

①

5.7

Mossy

NORTH EAGLE BEAK

Beak Job II 5.9
Begin on the obvious ramps in
the center of the north face.

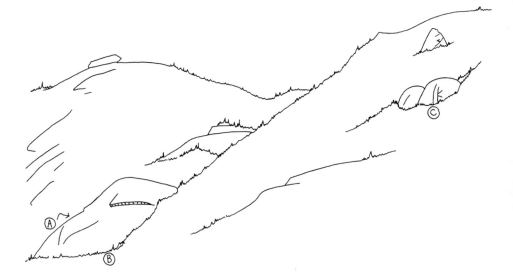

FALLEN EAGLE / THE EGGS

FALLEN EAGLE DOME
A   Amen III 5.8 A1
B   Let Us Thank Him II 5.7
   God Is Great II 5.8
   God Is Good II 5.9

THE NORTH EGG
C   Kind of Neat II 5.6

Approach   The approach to Fallen Eagle Dome and The Eggs is via the
Shuteye Pass trail from the east (the Mammoth Pool side).   Drive up the
Minarets Road from North Fork for 37 miles.   From a point 4 miles south of
Soda Springs Campground, a small sign marks the trail to Shuteye Pass.
Park here and hike up the trail for 1/2 hour. The climbs are easily seen from
the trail which passes close beneath the northeast face.   To approach The
Eggs, continue up the Shuteye Pass trail for another half mile.   Work up the
ridge to the north to the base of The Eggs and Kind of Neat.   It takes an extra
half hour past Fallen Eagle to reach The Eggs.

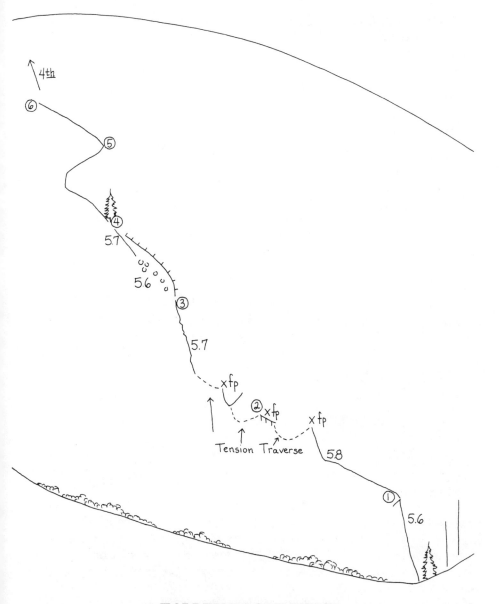

FALLEN EAGLE DOME

Amen III 5.8 A1
pro: double up on #3-#4 friends

FALLEN EAGLE DOME

A **Let Us Thank Him** II 5.7
B **God Is Great** II 5.8
C **God Is Good** II 5.9

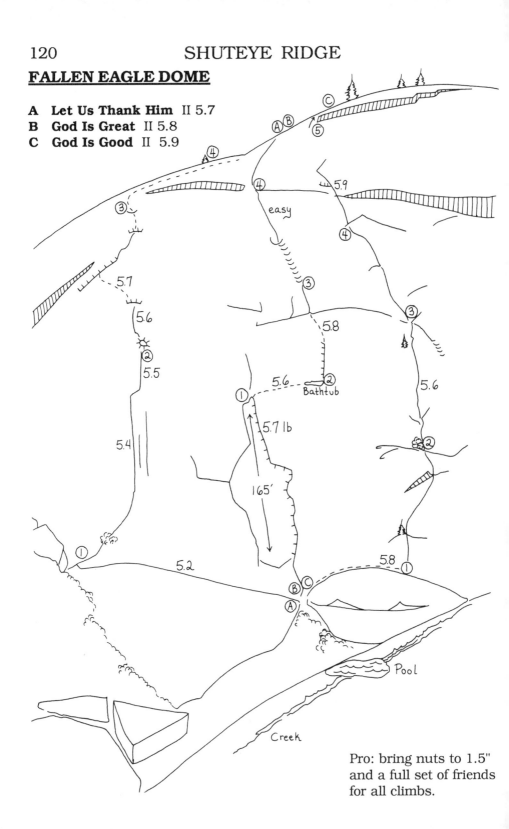

Pro: bring nuts to 1.5"
and a full set of friends
for all climbs.

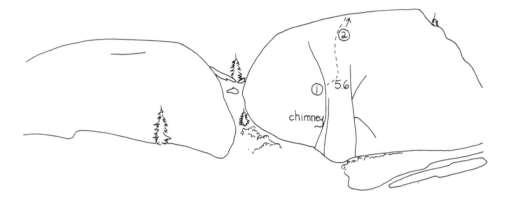

THE EGGS

THE NORTH EGG

Kind of Neat II 5.6
pro: set of friends

MINERVA DOME

A   Tail Feather III 5.8
B   Old Man's Dream III 5.9
C   Young Man's Fancy III 5.8
Bring protection to 4" for all climbs

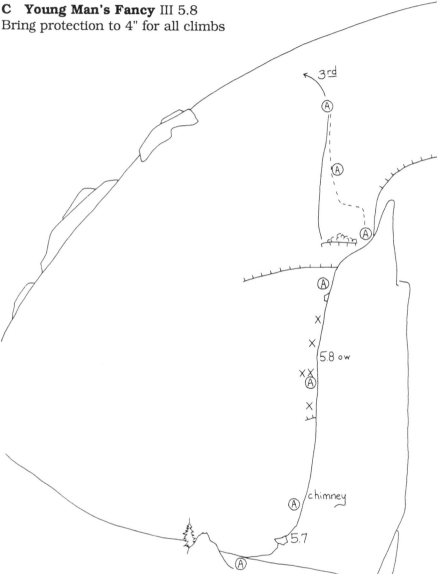

Wither II 5.10
Just south of Fernwood Alley, which separates Minerva Dome and Red Eagle
Dome is a green face. To the left of this face is a short corner facing north.
Traverse in from the right and climb up (5.10) until you can exit to a platform
on the left. From the platform climb up and left then straight up to a belay
ledge. Above, climb chickenheads up a small rib to the summit.

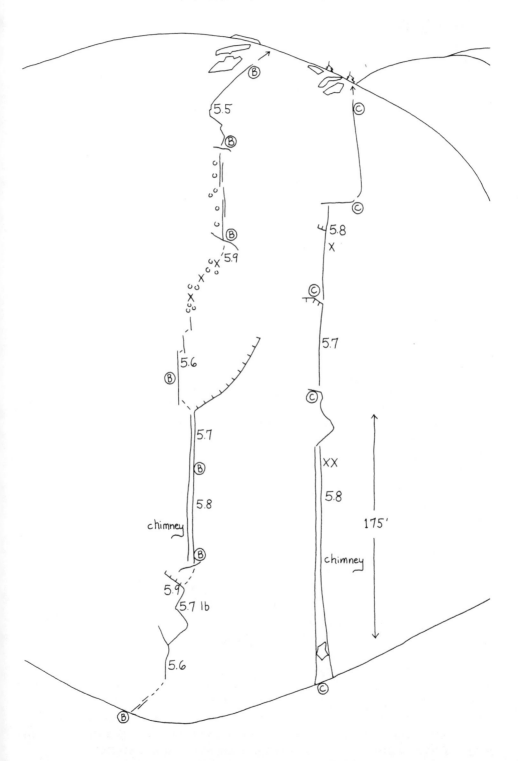

THE BASTION

The Bastion is the small cone-shaped dome
which is located up and behind Gray Eagle Dome.
The approach hike is the easiest from the Shuteye
Lookout above. However, the drive up the 4WD
road to the lookout can punish your car severely.
The approach is listed with the Shuteye Panorama on pages 112-113.

Acorn II 5.9
Begin in a squeeze chimney at the base of the east
face. Climb up and through two obstinate scrub
oaks. On the second pitch climb up the crux 5.9
jamcrack and past three loose blocks. On the
third pitch, climb past a short overhang and into
a low angle dihedral. Leave the dihedral via a fist
crack on the left and climb up the face near the
ridge to the summit.

RED EAGLE DOME

A **Triple Dihedral** II 5.8 pro: tiny to 2.5"
B **Red Dihedral** II 5.8 pro: include pro to 5", 6"

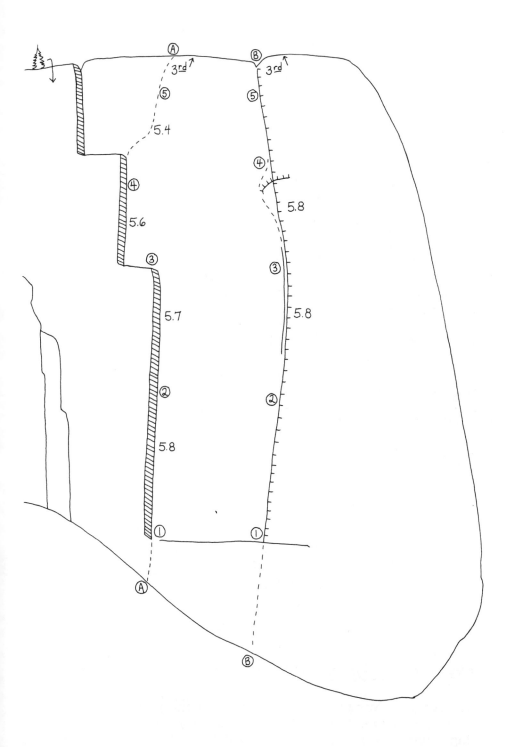

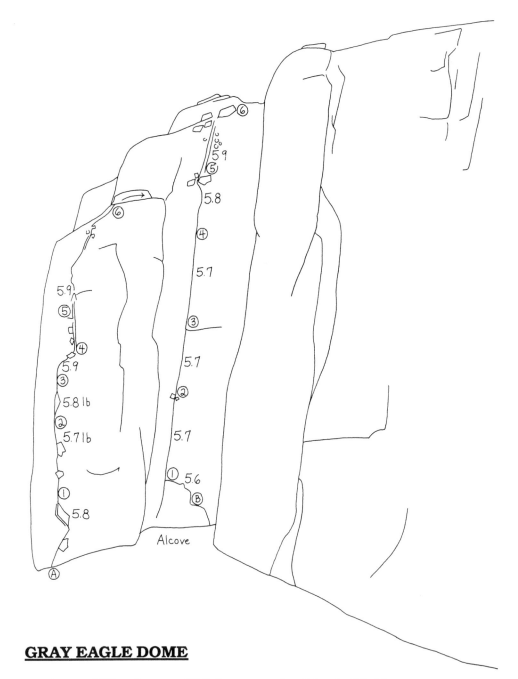

GRAY EAGLE DOME

A **Around The Corner** III 5.9   pro: extra friends #2-#4
B **The Great Depression** III 5.9   pro: nuts to 2", full set friends
C **Lightning Bolt** IV 5.8 A3   pro: kb's to 6" tubes

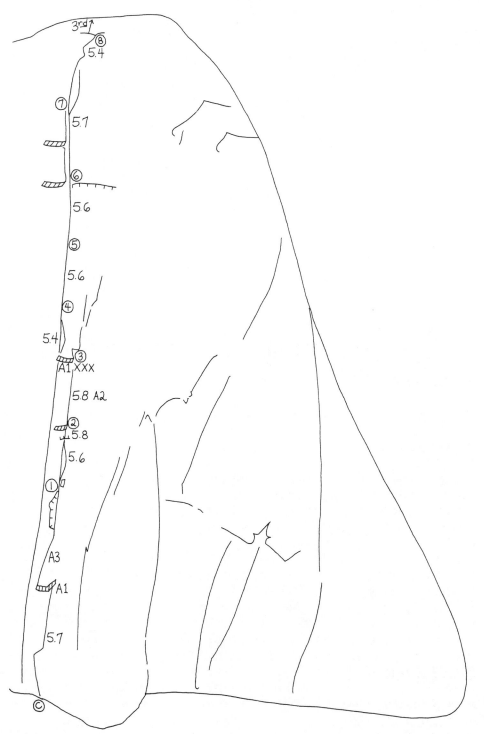

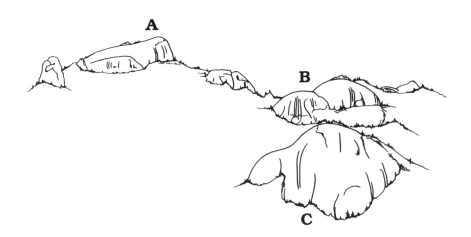

<u>SHUTEYE RIDGE - NORTHEAST</u>

A High Eagle Dome
B The Queens Throne
C Chiquito Dome (in the foreground, approach from Minarets Road)

Approach
Both High Eagle Dome and The Queens Throne are approached from the
Shuteye Lookout Road on the west side of Shuteye Ridge. From Bass Lake,
drive up the Beasore road for 10.3 miles to the junction of road 5S07 that
leads to Central Camp. Drive 5.1 miles on this dirt road to the junction of
road 6S42 to the Shuteye Lookout. Turn onto the Shuteye Lookout Road and
drive 3.6 miles. The road becomes rough and rocky, crossing 2 creeks before
reaching the junction of the Browns Meadow Road. The approach to The
Queens Throne begins at a logging spur just before reaching the Browns
Meadow Junction. To reach High Eagle Dome, follow the signs toward the
Shuteye Peak Lookout, 4 miles distant. Drive one mile up the deteriorating
road to the point where it turns 4WD at a gate. High Eagle Dome can be
identified as the large exfoliating dome rising above the road to the east. Park
here or just down the hill from the gate and hike down around the margin
of the northeast face to the start of the climbs. The road continues 3 more
miles to the lookout on top of Shuteye Peak. With a sturdy vehicle, you can
drive to the top and considerably shorten the approach to the Eagle Domes.

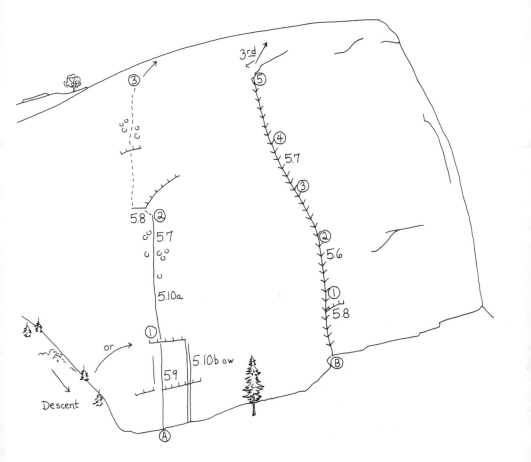

HIGH EAGLE DOME

A The Song of the Night II 5.10a
B East Crack II 5.8   Pro: to 3"

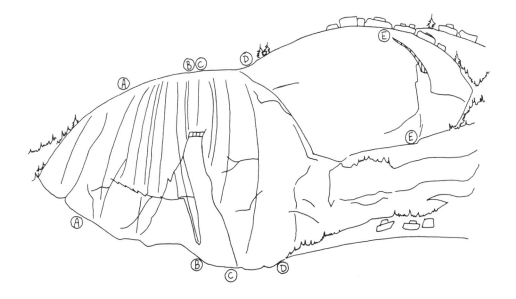

THE QUEENS THRONE

A A Climber's Requiem II 5.10b
B Scepter II 5.6
C The Pit and the Pendulum III 5.9 A2
D Coronet III 5.8
E Nipple By-Pass II 5.8

Approach From Bass Lake, drive up the Beasore road for 10.3 miles to the junction of road 5S07 that leads to Central Camp. Drive 5.1 miles on this dirt road to the junction of road 6S42 to the Shuteye Lookout. Turn onto the Shuteye Lookout road and drive 3.6 miles, crossing 2 creeks. Park at a logging spur just before the Browns Meadow road. Hike along this old logging road for 1/4 mile to an open meadow. The Queens Throne is visible just ahead. Drop down the margin of the east face to approach the climbs. The creeks in this section can be troublesome in the spring. Allow 15-20 minutes for the approach.

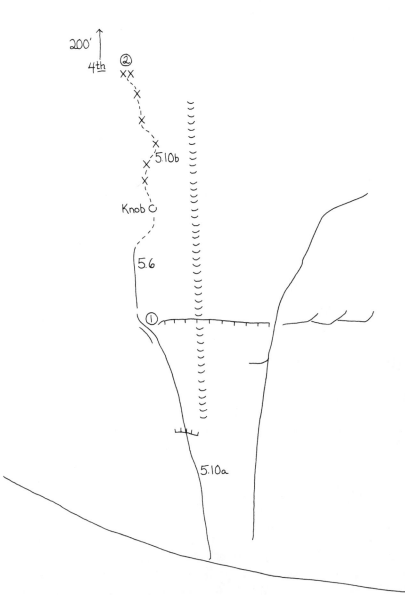

200'

4th

② XX

5.10b

Knob

5.6

①

5.10a

THE QUEENS THRONE

A Climber's Requium II 5.10b

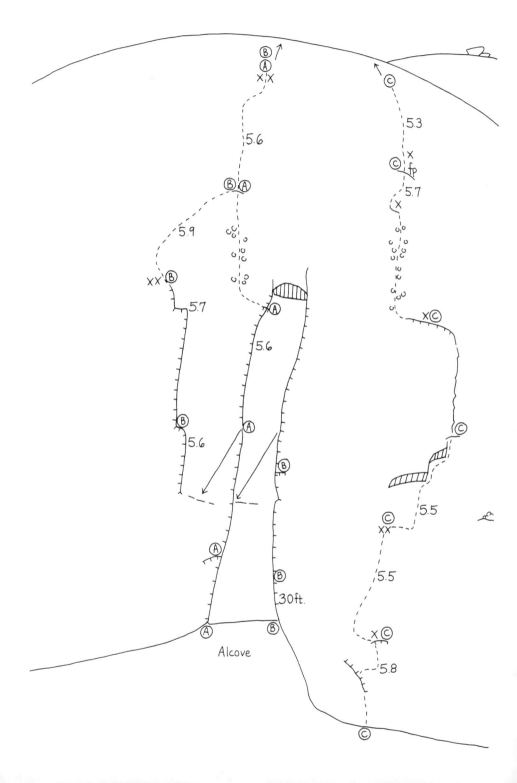

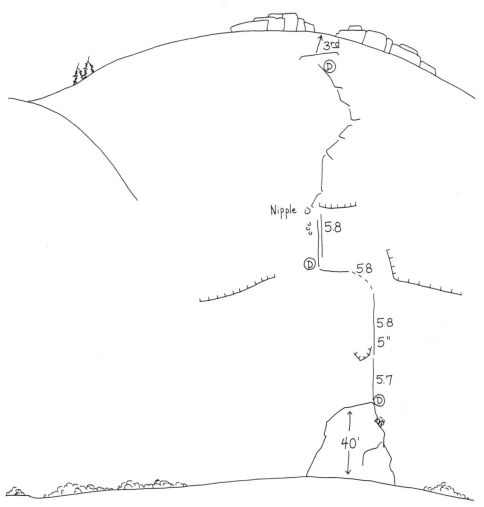

THE QUEENS THRONE

A **Scepter** II 5.6
B **The Pit and the Pendulum** III 5.9 A2
C **Coronet** III 5.8
D **Nipple By-Pass** II 5.8 Pro: to 4"

5.3
Left Water Crack
Made in the Shade

5.4
Big Dogs
Morning Thunder
Mt. Starr King-NE Face
Right Water Crack
Sink Me
Tin Roof
Worm Squirm

5.5
Eye of the Needle
First Lead
Mt. Starr King-SE Face
Opening Farewell
Trough
Walkabout
Woodchuck

5.6
Apple Ranch
Bay Bridge
Fox Trot
Fresno Dome-Arch Direct
Golden Toad-S Face Arch
Golden Toad-SW Ridge
Golden Toad-West Face
Green Slime
Kind of Neat
Nick Bottom
Night Driver
Scepter
Squaw Dome-West Book
Woodstock

5.7
Alcove Overhang
Aquarius
Cheeseburger in Paradise
Corporate Raiders
Dave's Breakfast
Double or Nothing
Fire and Ice
Five Years
Fresno Dome-South Pillar
Friction Dandy
Ghastly Gulch
Golden Gate
Hollow Wallow
Layaway Flake
Let Us Thank Him
Little Froggy
Looking Glass
Miwok
Mt. Starr King-East Face
Mule Train
Narley Waves
Niki's Nimbility
Nuthanger
Revenge of King Oscar
Shady Lane
Snowball
Split Decision
Sven and Yorgie
Tsunami
Walk We Crawl
Watership Down

5.8

Arch-A-Poko
Beagle Creeks
Big Country
Boulevard of Dreams
Busy Bee
Buzzard Book
Bypass
Cookie Slam
Coronet
Don't Look Back
Eye of the Toad
Fresno Flats
Glee
God Is Great
Good Book
Hanging Garden Crack
High Eagle Dome-Eest Crack
High Wire
Hot Tin Roof
Jigsaw Puzzle
Mt. Starr King-West Face
Nuts and Bolts
Old and Wise
Onyx
Red Dihedral
Rowsby Woof
Safe to Surf
Shakey Flakes
Sleeping Moss
Soft Shoe Shuffle
Stun 'Em With Science
Sword of Damocles-Right
Tail Feather
The Woods
Thin Spread
To Be Continued
Triple Dihedral
Water Wheel
West Fuller Butte-Easy Wind
Young Man's Fancy

5.9

Acorn
Archline
Around The Corner
Balloon Dome-East Face
Bare Minimum
Beak Job
Beast of Burden
Bell Bottom Blues
Boku-Muru
Bunnell Point-NW Face
Chulook
Circus of Values
Fresno Dome-Easy Wind
Galt's Gulch
God Is Good
Miranda
Mt. Starr King-NW Face
Odyssey
Old Man's Dream
On The Edge
Orange Peel
Snake Crack
Suicide Claim
Sword of Damocles-Left
The Acolyte
The Big Sleep
The Great Depression
Thunder Road
Vicious
Visions
Welcome to Wawona
White Dike

5.9+

Bad Animal
Eraserhead-The Prow
Impatience
Puck

5.10a

Betrayed
Blind Ambition
Color Me Gone
Hazy Days
Hole in the Wall
Lava Lamp
Rocky Road
Sphinx Crack
Talking Bear
Tempest Dome-Plate Route
The Song of the Night
Thompson Harmonizer
Wise Crack
Zephyr

5.10b

A Climber's Requium
Atlas
Chiquito Dome-South Chimney
Flamous
Hoser
Liberty
Mr. Toad's Wild Ride
Sahib
The Predator
Top Gun
Yellow Banana

5.10

Havana Ball
Nightwatch-Left Ski Track
Songs to a Morning Star
Wither

5.10c

Adrenaline Junkies
August Knights
Hula Hoop
Kammerlander
Meadow Rock-Lieback Route
Starched Shorts
That Little Strapless Number
Turning Green

5.10d

Panorama
Smith/Daughton
Voodoo Child

5.11a

Cornerstone
Easy Money
Elegance
Firefly
KOPA
Memphis Blues
Pipeline
Pyramamia

5.11b

Angel Wings
Atlantis
Blue Moon
Narrow Gauge

5.11c

Fear of Flying
Nubbs

5.11d

Aurora
Beat Farmer
Walk of Life

A1
Amen (5.8)
Routa de Fruta (5.8)
Pilgrims Progress
South Eagle Beak-East Face (5.8)
West Fuller Butte-East Face (5.9)

A2
Mammoth Pool Madness
East Fuller Butte-SE Face (5.8)
The Pit and the Pendulum (5.9)

A3
Balloon Dome-Beckey Route (5.8)
Lightning Bolt (5.8)
Balloon Dome-West Face (5.9)
Eagle Dihedral (5.9)

FIRST ASCENTS

MT STARR KING

Southeast Face II 5.5   George Anderson, James Hutchings,
   J.B. Lambert   1877
East Face II 5.7   John Roebig, Ron Schroeder, Tom Distler   7/69
Beast of Burden II 5.9   Mark Spencer   9/87
Tsunami II 5.7   Mark Spencer   9/87
Northeast Face II 5.4   George Bayley, E. S. Schuyler   1876
Northwest Face III 5.9   Ken Boche, Mary Bomba   9/70
Nuts and Bolts III 5.8   Tim Harrison, Ken Boche   1972
West Face III 5.8   Ken Boche, Lee Panza   5/70

Bunnell Point NW Face IV 5.9   Alan Bartlett, Robb Dillinger   6/83

WAWONA

LOWER FALLS

Hanging Garden Crack 5.8   Mark Spencer, Mark Etchell   2/84
Circus of Values 5.9   Mark Spencer   2/84
Angel Wings 5.11b   Mark Spencer, Floyd Hayes   7/85
Sphinx Crack 5.10a   Don Timmer   7/83

ICEHOUSE

Pilgrims Progress A1   Earl Tressenriter   7/62
Atlas 5.10b (Pilgrims Progress free)   Mark Spencer   6/87
Old and Wise 5.8   Earl Tressenriter   7/62   **FFA** Mark Spencer 6/82
Yellow Banana 5.10b   Mark Spencer, Mark Anderson   7/87
Cornerstone 5.11a   Mark Spencer, Dwight Simpson   7/87
Thompson Harmonizer 5.10a   Mark Spencer   3/84
Nubbs 5.11c   Mark Spencer   3/84
Double or Nothing 5.7   Mark Spencer   3/84
Galt's Gulch 5.9   Mark Spencer   3/84
Atlantis 5.11b   Mark Spencer   1/87
Color Me Gone 5.10a   Mark Spencer, Sean Nakamura,
   Dwight Simpson   6/87
Pyramania 5.11a   Mark Spencer   8/84

WAWONA DOME

Chulook II 5.9   Mark Spencer, Floyd Hayes   6/85
Boulevard of Dreams II 5.8   Mark Spencer, Jim Cunningham   10/86
Miwok II 5.7   Mark Spencer, Floyd Hayes   6/85
Hazy Days II 5.10a   Floyd Hayes, Kevin Wilcox, Mark Spencer   7/85
Welcome to Wawona II 5.9   Floyd Hayes, Kevin Wilcox   7/85
Beckey Route III 5.8 A2   Fred Beckey, Larry Moore,
   Bob Romanowitz   10/70

Blue Moon III 5.11b (Beckey Route free) Mark Spencer, Floyd Hayes 7/85
Tressenriter Capstone   Earl Tressenriter   1962
Hollow Wallow 5.7   Floyd Hayes, Scott Campbell   7/82

RIVER ROCK
Worm Squirm 5.4   Unknown
On The Edge 5.9   Mark Spencer   3/84
Alcove Overhang 5.7   Unknown   <1981
Green Slime 5.6   Unknown   <1981
Wise Crack 5.10a   Unknown   <1981
Firefly 5.11a   Unknown   <1981   **FFA** Mark Spencer   10/83
Sleeping Moss 5.8   Mark Spencer   10/83
Turning Green 5.10c   Mark Spencer   6/84

MEADOW ROCK
Bad Animal 5.9+   Unknown
Lieback Route 5.10c   Unknown   **FFA** Mark Spencer   10/83
Hula Hoop 5.10c   Mark Spencer   1/87

FRESNO DOME

HAWK DOME
Necromancy II 5.6   Erb, Max, Barney   8/73
Gypsy III 5.9   Erb, Sam, Fred   8/73
Raptor III 5.8   Max Gammon, Barney Neilson, Royal Robbins   8/73
Harlot II 5.6   Erb, Sam, Fred   8/73

ERASERHEAD
West Side 5.4   Brian Zane   8/83
Rocky Road 5.10a   Mark Spencer   7/83
Orange Peel 5.9   Mark Spencer   7/83
Shakey Flakes 5.8   Shirley Spencer   7/83
The Prow 5.9+   Mark Spencer   8/87
Cookie Slam 5.8   Mark Spencer   8/87
Tin Roof 5.4   Mark Spencer, Floyd Hayes   7/82

ECHO WALL
Big Dogs 5.4   Mark Spencer, Jim Cunningham   5/87
Woodchuck 5.5   Mark Spencer, Jim Cunningham   5/87
Split Decision 5.7   Jim Cunningham, Mark Spencer   5/87
The Woods 5.8   Max Gammon, Barney Neilson, Royal Robbins   8/73
Safe To Surf 5.8   Mark Spencer   6/87
Narley Waves II 5.7   Jim Cunningham, Mark Spencer   5/87
Pipeline II 5.11a   Mark Spencer   6/87

WEST FACE
Water Music II 5.8   Ruprecht Kammerlander, Tom Higgins   8/78
Kammerlander II 5.10c   Ruprecht Kammerlander, Tom Higgins   8/78
The Predator II 5.10b   Rockcraft Climbing School guides   mid 70s
Onyx II 5.8   Rockcraft Climbing School guides   mid 70s
Buzzard Book II 5.8   Fred Beckey, Jim Stuart   11/71
South Pillar II 5.7   Blaine Neeley, Randy Miller   7/85

SOUTH FACE
Easy Wind III 5.9   Mark Tuttle, Paul Loughton   1976
Mule Train II 5.7   Jim Cunningham, Tom Foll   7/87
Ghastly Gulch II 5.7   Randy Miller, Blaine Neeley, Dick Haskey,
   Carol LeMaster   6/85
Friction Dandy II 5.7   Blaine Neeley, Randy Miller   8/85
Looking Glass II 5.7   Unknown
Nuthanger II 5.7   R. Breedlove, J. Copeland, J. Day, R. Knehr   6/75
Rowsby Woof III 5.8   D. Erb, R. Fox   6/75
Watership Down III 5.7   M. Sorensen, R. Baum, R. Robbins   6/75
5.8 Offwidth 5.8   M. Sorensen, R. Baum, R. Robbins   6/75
Fresno Flats III 5.8   Unknown
Fox Trot II 5.6   C. Vandiver, M. Knehr, M. Potter   6/75

ZIPA-DE-DO-DA BUTTRESS
Bay Bridge 5.6   Royal Robbins et al   1973
Golden Gate 5.7   Royal Robbins et al   1973
Trough 5.5   Royal Robbins et al   1973
Busy Bee 5.8   Mark Spencer   10/87
Thin Spread 5.8   Royal Robbins et al   1973
Bypass 5.8   Royal Robbins et al   1973
Lay Away Flake 5.7   Royal Robbins et al   1973
Aurora 5.11d   Mark Spencer   10/87
Beat Farmer 5.11d   Lavon Weighall, Mark Spencer   10/87
Hole in The Wall 5.10a   Blaine Neeley   9/87
Snowball 5.7   Mark Spencer   10/87

PANORAMA WALL
Sink Me 5.4   Mark Spencer   7/87
Panorama 5.10d   Mark Spencer   5/87
Water Wheel 5.8   Mark Spencer   5/87
Fire and Ice 5.7   Mark Spencer   5/87
Morning Thunder 5.4   Mark Spencer   5/87

Made in the Shade 5.3   Mark and Shirley Spencer   4/87
Arch Direct 5.6   Blaine Neeley   1981

WILLOW CREEK WALL
Walk Of Life 5.11d Mark Spencer 6/86
Impatience 5.9+ Marty True, Mike Mayer 7/85
High Wire 5.8 Mark and Shirley Spencer 4/87
Starched Shorts 5.10c Mark Spencer, Jim Cunningham 6/86
Flamous 5.10b Mark Spencer 2/87
Talking Bear 5.10a Mark Spencer 4/86
Hoser 5.10b Mark Spencer, Dwight Simpson 8/86
Easy Money 5.11a Mark Spencer 2/87

THE BALLS

NIGHTWATCH
Arch-A-Poko II 5.8 Kirk Huizenga, Andy Belger, Cris Elisara 7/86
Left Ski Track II 5.10 Tom Higgins, Bob Kamps 8/76

THE GOLDEN TOAD
Mr. Toad's Wild Ride II 5.10b Dave Kelly, Dave Hoffman 7/85
Adrenaline Junkies II 5.10c Gary Fluitt, Randy O'Connell 7/85
Sven and Yorgie II 5.7 Gary Fluitt, Randy O'Connell 7/85
Eye of the Toad II 5.8 Hansel, Weidenhoffer, Gaffney
Revenge of King Oscar II 5.7 Gary Fluitt 7/85
West Face Route II 5.6 Unknown
Southwest Ridge II 5.6 Rick Vanderham 7/84
South Face Arch II 5.6 Unknown
Eye of the Needle II 5.5 Tim Hansel et al

TEMPEST DOME
Glee II 5.8 George Meyers, Mike Breidembach 5/76
Odyssey II 5.9 Tom Higgins, Shary McVoy, Alan Nelson 7/79
Plate Route II 5.10a Tom Higgins, Bob Kamps 8/76
Havana Ball II 5.10 Tom Higgins, Shary McVoy, Alan Nelson 7/79
Miranda II 5.9 Royal Robbins et al 1973
Little Froggy II 5.7 Jerry Koch, Jerry Boch 7/79
Shady Lane II 5.7 Bruce and Kathy McChubbrey 7/79

NO NAME RIDGE
Woodstock II 5.6 Unknown
Lava Lamp II 5.10a Unknown
To Be Continued II 5.8 Gary Fluitt, Niki Boughton 7/87

BOULDER GARDEN SLAB
Left Water Crack 5.3 Unknown
Right Water Crack 5.4 Unknown
First Lead 5.5 Unknown
Corporate Raiders II 5.7 Mark Spencer, Lavon Weighall 10/87
Big Country II 5.8 Lavon Weighall, Mark Spencer 10/87
Bare Minimum II 5.9 Bruce Wiede
Bell Bottom Blues II 5.9 Unknown
Hot Tin Roof II 5.8 Jeff Cooper
Aquarius 5.7 Mark Spencer 11/87
Night Driver 5.6 Mark Spencer 11/87

BOOK OF REVELATION
Niki's Nimbility II 5.7 Niki Boughton, Gary Fluitt 10/84
Dave's Breakfast II 5.7 Dave Mulky, Bill Pappas 7/85

MAMMOTH POOL

SQUAW DOME
Snake Crack II 5.9 Jack Delk, Guy McClure 7/77
West Book II 5.6 Tom and Karla DeSelms 6/84

DISSAPPEARING DOME
Memphis Blues IV 5.11a Steve McCabe, John Stoddard,
　　Mary Ellen Lawrence 10/78
Sword of Damocles - Left 5.9 John Stoddard, Mary Ellen Lawrence
　　1978
Sword of Damocles - Right 5.8 John Stoddard 1978

BALLOON DOME
Southeast Face Class 3 Alex LaPralty, Mel Lambertson 7/42
East Face III 5.9 Dave Black, Mike Graber 6/74
Boku-Muru III 5.9 Dave Black, Jim Black, Mike Graber 6/74
Beckey Route IV 5.8 A3 Fred Beckey, Reed Cundiff, Bill Hackett 6/71
West Face IV 5.9 A3 Dave Black, Jim Black, Mike Graber 6/74

WEST FULLER BUTTE
Breeze II 5.7 Fremont Brainbridge, Conrad VanBruggen, Gordon
Rhodes, Simon King 5/79
Walkabout II 5.5 Conrad Van Bruggen, Simon King,
　　Fremont Brainbridge, Mark Blanchard 5/77
Zephyr II 5.10a Steve McCabe, Gerri Dayharsh 6/79
Easy Wind II 5.8 Steve McCabe 7/77
East Face III 5.9 A1 Don Reid, Alan Bartlett 5/79

EAST FULLER BUTTE

Eagle Dihedral IV 5.9 A3   Jerry Coe, Galen Rowell   4/71
Smith / Daughton II 5.10d   Steve Smith, Tom Daughton   7/81
Narrow Gauge II 5.11b   Steve McCabe, Steve Smith   7/81
Southeast Face IV 5.8 A2   Fred Beckey, Jim Stuart, Walt Vennum,
  Greg Donaldson   5/72
Fear of Flying III 5.11c   Steve McCabe, John Stoddard   9/79
Songs to a Morning Star III 5.10   Mike Graber, David Black   11/74
White Dike II 5.9   Dave Black, Fred Beckey   4/75

JACKASS ROCK

Vicious II 5.9   Conrad Van Bruggen, Simon King, Fremont Brainbridge,
  Mark Blanchard   5/77
Don't Look Back II 5.8   Mark Spencer   10/87
Apple Ranch II 5.6   Mark Spencer, John Myers, Dan Abbott   8/80
Nick Bottom 5.6 Steve McCabe, Gerri Dayharsh, Jan Beyers   1977
Puck II 5.9+   Steve McCabe, Jeff Blanck   1977

MAMMOTH POOL DOME

That Little Strapless Number III 5.10c   Brett Bernhardt,
  Peter Carrick   7/86
Mammoth Pool Madness A2   Fremont Brainbridge,
  Conrad Van Bruggen   8/78

TRANQUILITY DOME

Visions III 5.9   Mark Blanchard, Conrad Van Bruggen, Simon King
  5/77
Suicide Claim III 5.9   Conrad Van Bruggen, Mark Blanchard,
  Fremont Brainbridge   8/83
Blind Ambition III 5.10a   Fremont Brainbridge, Conrad Van Bruggen
  8/78

CHIQUITO DOME

August Knights II 5.10c   Vaino Kodas, Patrick Paul   8/86
Sahib III 5.10b Tom Higgins, Cris Vandiver   7/83
Elegance III 5.11a   Tom Higgins, Cris Vandiver   11/80
KOPA 5.11a   Patrick Paul, Vaino Kodas   8/86
South Chimney III 5.10b   Jack Delk, Guy McClure   7/75
Top Gun III 5.10b   Greg Vernon, Blaine Neeley   7/86
Liberty III 5.10b   Blaine Neeley, Greg Vernon   7/86
Archline III 5.9   Fremont Brainbridge, Conrad Van Bruggen   5/79
The Acolyte II 5.9   Greg Vernon, J.D. Findley   9/86
Jigsaw Puzzle II 5.8   Conrad Van Bruggen, Simon King   5/78
Cheeseburger in Paradise II 5.7 Conrad Van Bruggen, Simon King 5/78

LETTERS TO PAUL
Betrayed 5.10a　　Skip Gaynard, Jack Delk, Ron Rockholt　6/86

SHUTEYE

THE QUEENS THRONE
A Climber's Requiem II 5.10b　　Herb Laeger, Eric Rhicard,
　　Greg Vernon　10/87
Scepter II 5.6　　Royal Robbins et al
The Pit and the Pendulum III 5.9 A2　　Royal Robbins et al
Coronet III 5.8　　Royal Robbins et al
Nipple By - Pass II 5.8　　Jack Delk, Sandy Schmeling　5/81

HIGH EAGLE DOME
East Crack II 5.8　　Jack Delk, Guy McClure　7/75
Song of the Night II 5.10a　　Eric Rhicard, Herb Laeger, Greg Vernon
　　10/87

GRAY EAGLE DOME
Around The Corner III 5.9　　Jack Delk, Ron Rockholt　5/87
The Great Depression III 5.9　　Jack Delk, Ron Rockholt　6/82
Lightning Bolt IV 5.8 A3　Jack Delk, Bill Sorensen, Skip Gaynard　6/79

RED EAGLE DOME
Triple Dihedral II 5.8　　Jack Delk, Guy McClure　6/76
Red Dihedral II 5.8　　Jack Delk, Bill Sorensen　7/78

MINERVA DOME
Tail Feather III 5.8　　Jack Delk, Guy McClure　6/77
Old Man's Dream III 5.9　　Jack Delk, Ron Rockholt　6/86
Young Man's Fancy III 5.8　　Jack Delk, Ron Rockholt　5/87
Wither II 5.10　　S. Sugine, R. Breedlove, Royal Robbins　1974

THE BASTION
Acorn II 5.9　　R. Breedlove, S Sugine, Royal Robbins　1974

THE EGGS
Kind of Neat II 5.6　　Jack Delk, Charles Knapp　5/86

FALLEN EAGLE DOME
Amen III 5.8 A1　　Jack Delk, Ron Rockholt　6/85
Let Us Thank Him II 5.7　　Jack Delk, Charles Knapp　5/85
God Is Great II 5.8　　Jack Delk, Sandy Schmeling, Ron Rockholt　4/85

God Is Good II 5.9 Jack Delk, Sandy Schmeling, Ron Rockholt 4/85

NORTH EAGLE BEAK
Thunder Road III 5.9 Conrad Van Bruggen, Simon King, Mark Blanchard 5/77
Beak Job II 5.9 Conrad Van Bruggen, Fremont Brainbridge, Simon King 6/80

SOUTH EAGLE BEAK
East Face II 5.8 A1 Hooman Aprin, Fred Beckey 10/72
Beagle Creeks II 5.8 Simon King, Conrad Van Bruggen, Fremont Brainbridge 5/82
Opening Farewell II 5.5 Fremont Brainbridge, Conrad Van Bruggen 6/81
Five Years II 5.7 Fremont Brainbridge, Conrad Van Bruggen 6/81

ROCK CREEK WALL
Walk We Crawl II 5.7 Mark Blanchard, Conrad Van Bruggen, Simon King 5/82
Soft Shoe Shuffle II 5.8 Mark Blanchard, Conrad Van Bruggen, Simon King 5/82

THE INCINERATOR
Routa de Fruta II 5.8 A1 Mark Blanchard, Simon King 10/82
Stun 'Em With Science II 5.8 Mark Blanchard, Jeff Panetta, Fremont Brainbridge, Simon King 9/82

BIG SLEEP DOME
The Big Sleep III 5.9 Doug Matthews, Steve McCabe 1979
Voodoo Child 5.10d Doug Matthews, Steve McCabe 1979

INDEX

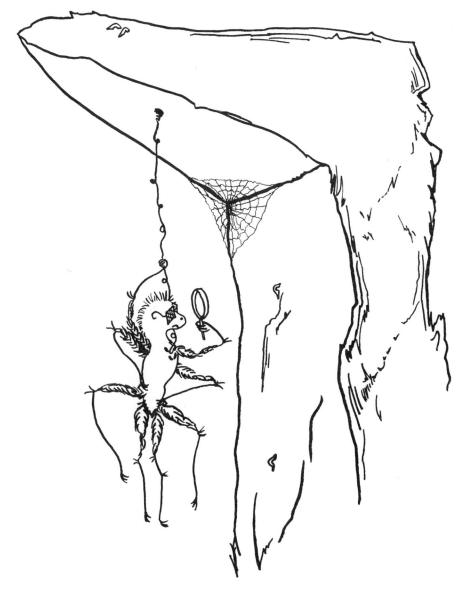

Spider Tricksters